1974   75-06445
                        75

B
JESUS   Longford, Frank
CHRIST   Pakenham, 7th...

            Jesus

DATE DUE

JESUS

A Life of Christ

JESUS
A Life of Christ

BY

LORD LONGFORD

Illustrated by

Richard Cuffari

DOUBLEDAY & COMPANY, INC.
GARDEN CITY, NEW YORK
1975

Library of Congress Cataloging in Publication Data

Longford, Frank Pakenham, 7th Earl of, 1905-
    Jesus: a life of Christ.

    First ed. published in 1974 under title: The life of Jesus Christ.
      Bibliography: p. 187
      1. Jesus Christ—Biography. I. Title.
BT301.2.L6   1975   232.9′01 [B]
ISBN 0-385-07008-X
Library of Congress Catalog Card Number 74-12698

To Elizabeth

ACKNOWLEDGMENTS

My first acknowledgment must be to my wife, who, for over forty years, has shared the studies and experiences on which this book is based: to Gwendolen Keeble, my personal assistant, Barbara Winch, Anne-Marie Obolensky, and Elizabeth Abbott, who typed the manuscript with sympathy and understanding. A first draft was shown to the Reverend Thomas Corbishley, S.J., and to the Reverend Eddie Stride and to Steve Stevens, dedicated evangelicals. Nearly all their suggestions were adopted, but none of them have any responsibility for the total outcome. A chronological note by Father Corbishley is appended.

The list of other friends from whom I have benefited must be endless, with a special place reserved for the Reverend Martin D'Arcy, S.J.

Biblical quotations were taken mainly from *The Holy Bible,* Revised Standard Version: Ecumenical Edition, but with free use of other versions.

Contents

Preface

Today hundreds of millions throughout the world are followers of Jesus Christ. He was born in or around 6 B.C. and crucified in or around April A.D. 30. He rose from the dead, so Christians believe, on the third day after his crucifixion and, forty days later, ascended into heaven. No human being has ever influenced world history so profoundly. But Christians believe he was not just a human being. He was at once man and God, with an unequaled spiritual message.

This duality in Jesus Christ's nature sets him apart from any other religious leader. Many millions follow the teachings of Buddha, Mahomet, and others. None of these leaders ever claimed divinity.

For over thirty years Jesus Christ lived on earth as a human being. He ate, drank, and slept as other humans. He experienced human emotions—anger, sorrow, and affection. His body was subject to human frailties, physical and emotional. In anticipation of his crucifixion he experienced extreme mental anguish. He died in the most appalling physical agony.

At the same time, Christ was fully aware of his divine nature and destiny: that he would dwell on earth for a short span, leaving a body of teachings that would last as long as human life on earth; that he would die on the cross for the salvation of mankind, and rise again from the dead.

* * *

But did it really happen? Or happen as Christians believe? This book is written from a broad Christian standpoint making, however, as few assumptions as possible based on faith rather than historical evidence. This evidence is basically to be found in the gospels, the four separate accounts of Christ's life written by the disciples, Matthew, Mark, Luke, and John, the evangelists.

By now it is barely possible for someone prepared to undertake the necessary research to doubt that the gospels were written within seventy years or so of the death of Christ, and that they give an honest picture of his life and message, as they were then understood.

It seems reasonable to date St. Mark's gospel between A.D. 65 and 70, thirty to forty years after the Crucifixion. St. John's gospel must have been produced before the end of the century. The gospels of St. Matthew and St. Luke come in between. Both rely heavily on St. Mark's gospel for their narrative facts and on a number of other sources then extant, written and oral, for their account of Jesus' teaching. The first epistles of St. Paul were written within about twenty years of the death of Jesus.

The gospels reflect an existing body of accepted fact and doctrine, as developed by the infant Church up to the time they were written. Jesus' sayings were first handed down mainly by word of mouth. The gospels themselves were either written by eyewitnesses or by people who had obtained their material from eyewitnesses. The authors were always in a position to draw fully on the common knowledge and understanding of the early Church. But the central belief, without which there would have been no Church and no gospel, was the belief that Jesus, having been put to death by crucifixion, rose from the dead.

It was for this belief that Peter and Paul, the two leading figures in the early Church, were crucified in Rome, probably by Nero, in A.D. 66 or 67; that is, before any of the gospels had been written. James, son of Zebedee and brother of John the evangelist, had been martyred for the same belief in Jerusalem by Herod Agrippa as early as A.D. 42, about twelve years after the death of Christ. The other apostles all faced the possibility of martyrdom in the same cause and most, as far as we can trace, underwent it. The apostles had the opposite of a vested interest in preaching aloud to all and sundry the gospel story; it was their certain passport to torture and execution.

In writing this book I have picked the brains of many, living and dead, who have given years of study to the life of Jesus Christ. I must ask forgiveness if I appear dogmatic at points where controversies have flourished and will always flourish. There is room for much difference of opinion about secondary matters. In regard to fundamentals, there is no need to hide one's convictions.

1
An Expectant People

Jesus was a Jew, a member of a people with a unique history that had already exhibited unique qualities. Their story up to the time of his birth was an extraordinary mixture of humiliation and glory.

The Jews were sustained by a conviction that two thousand years earlier, God had made a promise to their ancestor Abraham, since then repeatedly renewed. God had undertaken to treat them as his chosen people. The pact or covenant between God and Israel is the thread of continuity that runs through the Old Testament and leads on to the New.

The Old Testament makes up about two thirds of the Bible. It is, in the Christian view, a collection of divinely inspired writings concerning God's relationship with the people of Israel. The New Testament is concerned with Christ and Christianity. In the Old Testament the words of the prophets figure importantly—prophets spoke with divine inspiration on many subjects, not only about the future. In the Old Testament, God had said to Abraham: "Go from your country and your kindred and your father's house to the land that I will show you. And

I will make of you a great nation, and I will bless you, and make your name great, so that you will be a blessing. I will bless those who bless you, and him who curses you I will curse; and by you all the families of the earth shall bless themselves." The last few words pointed to their fulfilling a function of universal benefit; but the chosen people understood that long before that could happen it was their destiny to achieve preeminence.

The external facts of Jewish history since that time could be interpreted in more ways than one. Jesus lived his life in Palestine, a land of the Middle East, washed on the west side by the Mediterranean and divided throughout its length by the river Jordan. It lay at a crossroads where traffic routes and paths of invasion, the currents of civilization, all intersected. Abraham had entered this land, then called Canaan, as instructed, and he, his son Isaac, and his grandson Jacob had made it their home.

Jacob had twelve sons; one of them, Joseph, favored by his father, aroused the jealousy of his brothers, and they sold him into slavery in Egypt. There he rose to become the Pharaoh's right-hand counselor, and from that point of eminence was able to heap coals of fire on the brothers who had betrayed him. In a time of great famine he brought them and his old father Jacob to live in Egypt where, for many generations, they and their descendants prospered and multiplied.

But then came a time, perhaps four hundred years later, when Joseph had long been forgotten and the Israelites had fallen on evil days. Yet still their numbers increased. Pharaoh, King of Egypt, instructed the Hebrew midwives to kill all the male babies, to prevent a total Hebrew domination. Mercifully one "goodly child" was hidden in the bulrushes by his mother and rescued by Pharaoh's daughter. She called him Moses because, she said, "I drew him out of the water," and brought him up as her son. After many adventures Moses emerged as the divinely inspired deliverer of the people of Israel and led them out of Egypt in safety. After forty years' wandering in the wilderness, he brought them to the verge of Canaan, the promised land, the home of their ancestors.

By that time Moses had received many signs of divine favor, including the disclosure to him of the Ten Commandments and the whole new code of rules that came to be called the Mosaic Law. But in the eyes of the Lord, Moses' own fidelity had wavered in the desert. Moses was denied the supreme privilege of leading his people back into the promised land. He received every honor but that. "Moses," we are told, "went up from the plains of Moab to Mount Nebo, to the top of Pisgah, which is opposite Jericho. And the Lord shewed him all the land, Gilead as far as Dan, all Naphtali, the land of Ephraim and Manasseh, all the land of Judah unto the Western Sea, the Negeb, and the Plain, that is, the valley of Jericho, the city of palm trees, as far as Zoar." The Lord told him that this was the land about which he had made solemn promises to Abraham, Isaac, and Jacob. He had sworn to each one: "I will give it to your descendants." Now he had allowed Moses to see it unrolled in front of him. But that was all: "You shall not go over there."

So it was Joshua, Moses' successor, who led the people of Israel into Canaan in triumph. But it was not until after two hundred years of continuous struggle that a united kingdom was established. The author of this achievement was David, son of Jesse, a man of Bethlehem, in many eyes the most attractive figure in the Old Testament in spite of, or perhaps because of, his human frailties. He was originally introduced to King Saul as a young man whose skillful playing of the lyre could ease Saul's neurasthenia. David was accounted moreover "a man of valor, a man of war, prudent in spirit, and a man of good presence." The Lord was said to be with him. All this turned out to be true—somewhat too true for Saul's liking. David slaughtered the Philistine giant Goliath, and soon the people were chanting: "Saul has slain his thousands, and David his ten thousands." Saul turned violently against David, but Saul himself and his son, David's dear friend Jonathan, were slain by the Philistines in battle.

David succeeded to the leadership; the people rallied behind him. He made a "solemn" league with them at Hebron, where they anointed him King. He captured Jerusalem from the Jebusites, a tribe of Canaanites, making it his capital.

Some, at least, of the noblest psalms can be attributed to David, but his own morals were erratic. When he had committed adultery with the wife of Uriah the Hittite, one of his principal officers, he arranged for Uriah to lose his life in battle. He was accepted nonetheless in Jewish tradition as the founder of the royal house. The evengelists who concerned themselves with Jesus' genealogy (Matthew and Luke) were proud to trace it to David.

The period of freedom and unity was relatively brief. David's son Solomon, it is true, built a magnificent temple in which was lodged the "Ark," and showed many signs of excellence. God said to Solomon, "Behold, I give you a wise and discerning mind, so that none like you has been before you and none like you shall arise after you. I give you also what you have not asked, both riches and honor, so that no other king shall compare with you all your days." But the end was not so happy. We are told that his love for foreign women—he had seven hundred wives and three hundred concubines—proved his undoing. "Now King Solomon loved many foreign women; the daughter of Pharaoh, and Moabite, Ammonite, Edomite, Sidonian and Hittite women, from the nations concerning which the Lord had said to the people of Israel: 'You shall not enter into marriage with them, neither shall they with you, for surely they will turn away your heart after their gods'; Solomon clung to these in love." Nevertheless, in the eyes of his people he died an old and honorable man.

On his death, however, the ten northern tribes set up a separate kingdom under the name of Israel, leaving the two southern ones to form the state of Judah, which included Jerusalem. Both kingdoms were gradually destroyed by external aggression. The first Assyrian invasion of Israel took place in 732 B.C.; the kingdom collapsed twelve years later. A century and a half later, in 586 B.C., Judah underwent the same fate, this time at the hands of Babylon. A revolt was mercilessly crushed. The populations in each case were largely deported— in the case of Judah to Babylon. Four hundred years after the death of David, the chosen people had virtually disappeared from the chosen territory.

But Babylon, in its turn, fell before Persia. Cyrus, the new ruler, gave foreigners leave to return to their homelands (538 B.C.). It was not until about 400 B.C., however, that under the prophet Ezra the Jews returned in large numbers, full of re-forming zeal. Their confidence in the divine promises had waxed rather than waned during their two hundred years of exile. But in that time they had worked out a rigid system of legalism, narrowly exclusive of non-Jews, and a general out-look of "religious nationalism."

The Persian domination went the way of the others. The Persian empire was conquered by Alexander the Great in about 320 B.C., and Palestine became a Greek territory. When Alex-ander died, his Asian territories were divided between the Lagid dynasty, based on Egypt, and the Seleucids, based on Syria. Palestine was allocated to the former, but about 200 B.C. they were defeated and supplanted by the Seleucids. The new rulers carried out a policy of brutal repression, and made every effort to extinguish the powerful Jewish religion, but the Jew-ish people showed no sign of apostasy. Their resistance under the heroic leadership of the family of Maccabees turned into a fierce war for independence.

A guerrilla struggle was carried on with the utmost ruthless-ness until the Greek rulers gradually capitulated. In 166 B.C. religious freedom was conceded and political freedom in 129 B.C. But, as on other occasions in Jewish history, the fruits of glorious self-sacrifice were thrown away through internal dissension. The Romans, eagerly extending their dominions in the east, found a ready excuse for interference. In 63 B.C.

Pompey breached the walls of Jerusalem after a three-month siege. Palestine was annexed and became a Roman vassal. Throughout Christ's life, that was her status: She was more like a modern colony than an occupied territory.

The Romans made use of local kings or tetrarchs and, on a lower level, of "publicans" or tax collectors, who were detested as quislings by the Jewish population. They allowed the Jews a certain amount of religious autonomy, but very much on Roman terms. In a period of fifty years, no less than eight high priests who did not suit the Romans were gotten rid of. The latter held the Jews in contempt, and the Jews in their turn felt contempt for the Romans (using the word "contempt" in a more religious sense). Whatever the physical facts might suggest, the Jews believed, as they were later to tell Jesus, that they had never "been in bondage to any man."

In 40 B.C., Herod, an Idumean of a Bedouin family, the "mayor of the palace," assumed the crown of David through the decision of Mark Antony and Octavius Caesar. His reign, lasting thirty-six years, was marked by unrestrained brutality and tyranny, but was not without a certain grandeur. On the whole it was a period of prosperity for the Jews. Herod left behind him a great marble palace, the fortress Antonia, and the huge restored temple, which far surpassed the original edifice of Solomon in size and costliness.

He was still alive at the time of Jesus' birth and just had time to massacre the innocent babies of the Bethlehem area before he died in 4 B.C. He had had numerous children by his various wives but had had most of the children put to death. Only four sons survived, and his territory was divided among them, although the total power allowed them did not add up to what his had been. When Jesus was growing up, Palestine, a country smaller than Belgium, with a population of less than one million, was divided into three parts. Herod Philip II was officially tetrarch (but often called King) of Iturea and Trachonitis; Herod Antipas, generally called Herod in the gospels, was tetrarch of Galilee and Perea; but the dominant figure was the Roman procurator of Judea, a province formerly under the rule of another of Herod the Great's sons, Archelaus. The procurator controlled matters throughout the whole area when he judged it necessary, either from Jerusalem or from his more usual place of residence at Caesarea on the coast. Pontius Pilate was the fifth such procurator.

The people of Israel, within their own sphere of life, were a theocracy. At their head was the high priest who came, through his religious pre-eminence, to be looked on as the political leader of the Jewish community. He was surrounded by a vast number of priests, Levites (a somewhat lower order), and lesser figures. Out of that small population twenty-five thousand men were employed in the temple, but the public influence of the priesthood had been much diminished since the coming of the "scribes."

The scribes, originating during the Babylonian exile, had become expert in interpreting the minutiae of the law and by Jesus' time were a more potent force than the official priests. The two groups—priests and scribes—were both represented in the Sanhedrin, a body seventy-strong that had the supreme voice in matters involving both religion and politics.

But there is another distinction to be noted. We read of the scribes and Pharisees, but also of the Pharisees and Sadducees. The category of Pharisees overlapped that of the scribes, but many Pharisees were not scribes but belonged to the humbler orders of society, and many scribes were certainly not Pharisees. The Pharisees were remarkable for the meticulous austerity of their personal lives and for their ever stricter understanding and application of the Mosaic Law. The Sadducees, representing a wealthier element, were conservative in more ways than one. They were fastidious if not fanatical in their interpretation of the law; they were unsympathetic to what they regarded as new-founded notions like belief in the after-life. The Pharisees, to their credit, had done much to keep alive the national spirit of religion in face of alien oc-

cupation. The Sadducees were more ready to do business with
the Roman authorities.

*   *   *

So, conquered in turn by Babylon, Assyria, more than one
Greek dynasty, and now the Romans, Palestine had enjoyed
no more than sixty-five years of independence out of the previous six hundred. This catalogue of suffering and subordination
might seem to discredit the persistent claim to divine favor.
But just as easily, it could be argued that a people that had
undergone such shattering experiences, and yet maintained its
spirit and confidence so completely unshaken, must possess a
secret not readily apparent to the outward eye.

Apparent or not, the Jews did possess an inner source of
strength and moral indestructibility. They had their law and
their covenant with God, and linked with that a tremendous
hopefulness. Their law might have been, no doubt was, capable of becoming a caricature of itself. It involved a mass of
observances that to many of us seem strange. The total doctrine had come to include a body of ethical teaching and spiritual awareness that has stood the test of time.

In the beginning, faithfulness to the national creed and the
denial of idols had seemed sufficient. Then came the Ten Commandments and other ethical instructions. Then a profound
moral transformation exemplified in the prophetic books and
the other sacred writings. No Christian has ever failed to draw
strength from such a psalm as the *Miserere:*

Have mercy on me, O God,
according to thy steadfast love;
according to thy abundant mercy
blot out my transgressions.
. . . For thou hast no delight in sacrifice;
were I to give a burnt offering,
thou would'st not be pleased.
The sacrifice acceptable to God is a broken spirit;
a broken and contrite heart, O God, thou wilt not despise.

We shall find that Jesus Christ laid great emphasis on the nobler aspects of Old Testament teaching. "Think not," said Jesus Christ, "that I have come to abolish the law and the prophets. I have come not to abolish them but to fulfill them . . . till heaven and earth pass away, not an iota, not a dot, will pass from the law until all is accomplished." Admittedly he proceeded at once to expound a new version of the law that went wider and deeper than the old in many respects. Yet the old never lost its significance.

What Jesus called the first two commandments, "You shall love the Lord your God . . . and your neighbor as yourself," are derived from the traditional Jewish law, though in the parable of the good Samaritan, Jesus did demonstrate an altogether new meaning of the word "neighbor."

Neither then nor afterward at any time did he repudiate or disparage the law as the foundation and starting point of true theology and ethics.

The covenant with God and the sense of special election gave rise to an unwavering and increasing hopefulness. The Israelites, after all, were the chosen people. True, they had repeatedly gone wrong, either collectively or through their rulers. Moses, David, and Solomon, to mention only the greatest, had been punished for their errors. Moses had been favored by God as no other figure in the Old Testament: We are told that the Lord spoke to him as if they were friends. But he had not been allowed to enter the Holy Land. David had gone astray. Solomon, for all his renowned wisdom, had proved himself terribly self-indulgent.

Yet the Israelites could attribute their misfortunes to their own sinfulness without disturbing their assurance that the promises were theirs for the asking, when they proved worthy. Not for one moment did they suppose that they had blotted their copybook so irretrievably as to forfeit their birthright. They were convinced beyond argument that their time would come.

But this immense all-sustaining hope, nurtured by a succession of prophets whose mission had been to fortify and succor the soul of the people, was as vague as it was far-reaching. A central place in their expectations became associated with a marvelous being, the Lord's anointed, who would come to end the sufferings of Israel—in Aramaic "Meschiah," in Greek "Christos." The title and the dream permitted quite contradictory, often ambiguous, interpretations, being applied variously to a king, a priest, and a patriarch. Only the prophet Daniel used it in the modern sense.

* * *

Profound interest has been aroused in recent years by the discovery of the Dead Sea Scrolls, manuscripts that have come to light since 1947 in a number of areas northwest of the Dead Sea. They derive from a point in time hundreds of years earlier than the earliest of the Old Testament manuscripts.

The scrolls lay bare the life of the Essenes of the Qumran community, monks living within rules of extreme asceticism. It is uncertain whether the Qumran community had any influence on the early Christians. So far no definite evidence has emerged that either Jesus Christ or John the Baptist had any contact with them, although this is more likely to have been true of John the Baptist than Jesus.

The Qumran community certainly entertained a messianic expectation. In the words of Professor F. F. Bruce, "The Qumran community and the early Christians agreed that there would arise a great prophet, a great captain and ruler, and a great priest." But these figures remained distinct in Qumran expectation, whereas the early Christians saw them united in the person of Christ.

Despite all the ambiguities and inconsistencies, the conviction of the Jews was unanimous that a messiah of some kind would arise in due course to end the sufferings of Israel.

John the Baptist, often called "the forerunner," was asked

this question before all others: "Are you the Messiah?" Even in Samaria, the woman with whom Jesus spoke at the well said with confidence: "I know that the Messiah is coming, he who is called Christ. When he comes, he will show us all things." This intense expectation was reaching a peak at the time of Jesus' birth. If and when he put himself forward as a messiah, Jesus would be speaking to a people who were ready and waiting.

There is debate as to how far the actual role of Christ could be deduced from Old Testament prophecies.

Certainly there are passages of striking significance in the light of hindsight. When the three wise men came to Jerusalem and put the question: "Where is he who has been born King of the Jews?" the chief priests and scribes had no difficulty in giving them and Herod the answer. Christ, they said, was to be born in Bethlehem, "for so it is written by the prophet:

> And you, O Bethlehem, in the land of Judah,
> are by no means least among the rulers of Judah;
> for from you shall come a ruler
> who will govern my people Israel."

One view is that only Christian faith could have enabled anyone to recognize Christ from the prophetic descriptions. Against that is the reference to a messiah who comes riding in humility on an ass and the foal of an ass, and the famous passage from Isaiah 53 shows a true prefiguration of the sacrifice of Calvary:

> He was despised and rejected by men;
> a man of sorrows, and acquainted with grief;
> and as one from whom men hide their faces,
> he was despised, and we esteemed him not.
> Surely he has borne our griefs
> and carried our sorrows;
> yet we esteemed him stricken,
> smitten by God, and afflicted.

> But he was wounded for our transgressions,
> he was bruised for our iniquities;
> upon him was the chastisement that made us whole,
> and with his stripes we are healed.

But between the concept of a suffering servant redeeming mankind through his afflictions on the one hand, and that of a victorious king on the other, the popular choice was always likely to favor the glorious exemplar of worldly success.

And so it happened. The suffering servant of the second Isaiah, which has acquired so much significance in Christian thought, was lost sight of till after Calvary. When Christ announced himself as heralding and introducing the kingdom of God, he found a multitude of ready listeners. At least one meaning of his words was entirely consistent with contemporary opinion. But what was being awaited was a terrestrial rather than a spiritual king, a worldly rather than a heavenly kingdom. There lay in store a great and painful awakening.

2
The Hidden Years

The prophet Isaiah had foretold six or seven hundred years earlier that when the Messiah was about to arrive, he would be preceded by a mighty forerunner. A voice would be heard crying in the wilderness:

Prepare the way of the Lord,
make his paths straight.
Every valley shall be filled
and every mountain and hill shall be brought low, . . .
And all flesh shall see the salvation of God.

About A.D. 26, the voice of John the Baptist was heard saying these words in the wilderness east of Judea, beyond the Jordan. He made an arresting impression even on the Jews, who were long accustomed to prophets. He wore a garment of camel hair and a leather girdle around his waist, and ate locusts and wild honey. Indeed, he was dressed in a style that deliberately recalled Elijah himself. Large numbers flocked to hear him and were baptized in the Jordan, confessing their sins. From the first, the heart of John's message lay in his call to repentance; the symbol of it was his baptism with water. He contrasted this sharply with the coming of the Messiah, which would be with fire and the Holy Spirit, and bring new life to the soul.

John was severe and uncompromising toward the Pharisees and the Sadducees. It is interesting that not a few of these did in fact come to him for baptism. Some of them at least received an explosive reception. "You brood of vipers," he called them. "Who warned you to flee from the wrath to come? Bear fruits that befit repentance, and do not begin to say to yourselves, 'We have Abraham as our father'; for I tell you, God is able from these stones to raise up children to Abraham." The populace seemed to expect and even to relish this kind of language. In general they heard him gladly, and asked, "What then shall we do?" His moral guidance was clear if limited. "He who has two coats, let him share with him who has none. And he who has food, let him do likewise." Tax collectors were told to collect no more than the appointed sum. To soldiers he said, "Rob no one by violence or by false accusation, and be content with your wages."

But his message was not only an ethical one. It held out an immediate and dramatic prospect. When asked whether he himself was the Christ, he returned an emphatic negative. He told them explicitly: "He who is mightier than I is coming, the thong of whose sandals I am not worthy to untie; . . . His winnowing fork is in his hand, to clear his threshing floor, and to gather the wheat into his granary, but the chaff he will burn with unquenchable fire." We are left in no doubt whatever that what he preached was "good news to the people."

One day there came from Nazareth in Galilee, some seventy miles away, a young man aged about thirty-three, whose name was Jesus. John was Jesus' cousin, but he and John had probably not met for some time. One can assume, however, that John recognized Jesus instantly. A sign from heaven seems to have assured John of the divine element in Jesus. When Jesus asked to be baptized, John checked him: "I need to be baptized by you, and do you come to me?" Jesus gently but firmly set the objection aside. "Let it be so now," he said, "for thus it is fitting for us to fulfill all righteousness." John gave way and performed the ceremony. When Jesus emerged from the water after baptism, the spirit of God descended like a dove upon him, and a voice was heard from heaven saying: "This is my belóved son, with whom I am well pleased."

Here was not the beginning but the culmination of the relationship between the forerunner and the Messiah. It had begun over thirty years earlier, before either of them was born.

* * *

There lived at that time an aged priest called Zechariah. He and his wife Elizabeth were renowned for their outstanding piety, but they were elderly people, and up to this point she was barren. There seemed no hope of a child.

One day when his division of the priesthood was on duty, Zechariah, according to custom, entered the temple to burn incense while the people prayed outside. "And there appeared to him an angel of the Lord." "When men," wrote the late Archbishop Temple, "see or hear angels, it is to be supposed that an intense interior awareness of a divine message leads to the projection of an image which is then experienced as an occasion of something seen and heard. We need not suppose," he adds, "that they took physical form, so that all who 'saw' anything must see the same thing."

This angel's name was Gabriel. Zechariah was awestruck, but the angel said to him: "Do not be afraid, Zechariah, for your prayer is heard, and your wife Elizabeth will bear you a son, and you shall call his name John." Their son would "turn many" to the Lord and would go before him "in the spirit and power of Elijah." He would make ready the people to receive the Lord.

Zechariah expressed bewilderment, bordering on disbelief, in view of the advanced years of himself and Elizabeth. The angel assured him, however, that all this would indeed happen, though Zechariah himself would be punished for his skepticism by being struck dumb for a period. All happened as foretold. Zechariah emerged from the temple dumb. Elizabeth conceived and cried out in gratitude: "Thus the Lord has done to me in the days when he looked on me, to take away my reproach among men." For five months she hid herself from the public gaze.

In the sixth month of her confinement, the same angel Gabriel descended upon Nazareth, a village of Galilee, and appeared to Mary, a relation of Elizabeth's, "a virgin betrothed to a man named Joseph."

Jewish matrimony was completed in two stages. First came the betrothal, which represented a binding contract, though sexual relations were not yet permitted. Then about a year later came the marriage feast; the bride was taken into the bridegroom's house and full married life ensued. At the time of the visitation by the angel, Mary was passing through the first stage.

Both Joseph and Mary could trace remote descent from King David and belonged therefore to the royal house of Israel. But there was no doubt about their poverty. Joseph was an artisan, presumably a carpenter, though he probably performed other tasks. When Jesus was born, they could only afford a pair of turtledoves for their prescribed offering to the temple. A lamb was expected from anyone of means. Joseph must have been at least twenty-five; Mary according to local custom would have been quite a few years younger, possibly no more than fifteen.

"Hail, O favored one," said the angel to Mary, "the Lord is with you." Mary was bewildered, as Zechariah had been. But the angel set her fears at rest. "Do not be afraid, Mary," he said, "for you have found favor with God." She would conceive a son; she was to give him the name of Jesus. He would be called the Son of the Most High. The Lord God would give him the throne of his father David. He would reign over the House of Jacob forever. There would be no end of his kingdom.

Zechariah had pointed to the great age of his wife and himself as obstacles to the fulfillment of the promise. Mary was also puzzled, though here there was no element of disbelief. She pointed out that she had no husband. How then could she have a child? Gabriel replied with the stupendous explanation: "The Holy Spirit will come upon you, and the power of the Most High will overshadow you." Therefore the child to be born would be called holy, the Son of God. The virgin would remain a virgin always. Mary's response was immediate and total. "Behold, I am the handmaid of the Lord; let it be to me according to your word." The angel departed, leaving her with this infinite prospect.

The angel had told her what presumably had not reached her ears, that the elderly Elizabeth had astonishingly conceived a son and was in her sixth month of confinement. Mary set off to make the long journey to Ain Karim, the town in the Judean hills where Elizabeth was living in retirement. Mary greeted Elizabeth and at once the baby that was to be John the Baptist leaped in the womb. Elizabeth was filled with the Holy Spirit and exclaimed, with a loud cry: "Blessed are you among women, and blessed is the fruit of your womb." She added words that we must attribute to inspiration. "And why is this granted me, that the mother of my Lord should come to me?" And with clear reference to Mary's unquestioning acceptance of her divine vocation: "And blessed is she who believed that there would be a fulfillment of what was spoken to her from the Lord." Mary replied with the immortal song of praise that we call the *Magnificat:*

My soul magnifies the Lord,
and my spirit rejoices in God my Savior,
for he has regarded the low estate of his handmaiden.
For behold, henceforth all generations will call me blessed;
for he who is mighty has done great things for me,
and holy is his name.
And his mercy is on those who fear him

from generation to generation.
He has shown strength with his arm,
he has scattered the proud in the imagination of their hearts,
he has put down the mighty from their thrones,
and exalted those of low degree;
he has filled the hungry with good things,
and the rich he has sent empty away.
He has helped his servant Israel,
in remembrance of his mercy,
as he spoke to our fathers,
to Abraham and his posterity forever.

Mary remained with Elizabeth about three months, and then returned to her home.

In due course John was born amid general rejoicing. The relatives and neighbors wanted him to be called Zechariah after his father, but his mother would have none of it. "Not so," she said, "he shall be called John." But why, they asked? None of his relations had that name. She remained adamant. Zechariah, still deprived of speech, was consulted in sign language. He called for a writing tablet and gave a definitive ruling. "His name is John." The company, knowing nothing of the angel's instructions, could only marvel. Far and wide throughout the hill country went the story of these occurrences. People began to ask themselves what this child would be. The hand of the Lord was clearly upon him.

Zechariah, his power of speech restored, gave vent to a tremendous utterance.

Blessed be the Lord God of Israel,
for he has visited and redeemed his people,
and has raised up a horn of salvation for us
in the house of his servant David,
as he spoke by the mouth of his holy prophets from of old,
that we should be saved from our enemies,
and from the hand of all who hate us; . . .

He reaffirmed the confidence of himself and his people in the holy covenant between God and Abraham and addressed himself directly to his new-born child.

And you, child, will be called the prophet of the Most High,
for you will go before the Lord to prepare his ways,
to give knowledge of salvation to his people
in the forgiveness of their sins.

Legend has inspired a great painter in Poussin to picture Elizabeth bringing John, still a little child, to visit Mary and Jesus. In the gospels, however, we do not hear any more of John for over thirty years, when we encounter him as the fierce prophet in the wilderness.

We now turn from a human to a divine nativity.

＊ ＊ ＊

"In those days," says St. Luke, "a decree went out from Caesar Augustus that all the world should be enrolled—that is, that a complete census should be carried out. This must fairly certainly have been somewhere between 8 and 4 B.C., with the date of 6 B.C. the most likely. Joseph and Mary were required by their membership, however remote and humble, of the royal house of David to register in Bethlehem, which was David's birthplace.

When it had become known some months previously that Mary was pregnant, Joseph—well aware that he had played no part in the pregnancy—was anxious to cause her the minimum of shame and to set aside the marriage contract as quietly as possible. But an angel had reassured him in a dream. He need not fear to take Mary for his wife. "That which is conceived in her is of the Holy Spirit." She would bear a son who must be given the name of Jesus, "for he will save his people from their sins." We are reminded by St. Matthew of the prophecy of Isaiah: "Behold a virgin shall conceive and bear a son, and his name shall be called Emmanuel" (a word meaning "God with us"). Joseph willingly did as he was told: "He took his wife," but without physical consummation.

Now the little party, Joseph, Mary, and the child within her, set out on the journey from Nazareth to Bethlehem, about seventy-five miles over inadequate roads. It would take at least four days, with Mary being jolted up and down on the back of an ass. No laughing matter for a pregnant woman. They would cross the plain of Esdralon and Samaria before entering Judea, harsh and bitter in its physical aspect compared with smiling Galilee, even though the inhabitants of Judea despised the Galileans.

Every Jewish heart would swell with emotion at the sight of Jerusalem and the temple that Herod, here at least a benefactor, had rebuilt in glorious dimensions. After two more hours traveling they would reach Bethlehem, a little white town situated on twin hills with perhaps two thousand inhabitants. Mary and Joseph, who alone shared the secret of the divine destiny of Mary's child, would not be likely to forget the prophecy of Micah that a ruler of Israel would come out of Bethlehem.

The birth of Christ can fairly be described as the most momentous event in human history. The actual scene has inspired unlimited art and legend, but the gospel narration is brief and bald. While Joseph and Mary were in Bethlehem "the time came for her to be delivered. And she gave birth to her firstborn son and wrapped him in swaddling clothes, and laid him in a manger, because there was no place for them in the inn."

The inn was probably a type of caravansary still found in oriental countries. There would have been a square enclosure open to the sky for the sheep and cattle, with a wooden porch providing some sort of cover for human beings, and a few rooms to be rented at exorbitant prices. Bethlehem would have been full of nomads engaged in primitive forms of trade and of course a large inflow of visitors for the census. The stable in which Jesus was born was almost certainly a cave of a kind that was used and is still used to shelter sheep and cattle. The ox and the ass that we traditionally place on either side of the crib are apocryphal rather than historical, but few Christians would wish to abandon the picture of these humble beasts of burden present at the birth of the Redeemer.

Interpreters of the life of Christ vary from those who see at every moment a direct intervention by providence to those, including the present writer, who draw on such explanation sparingly. It is difficult, however, not to feel that the utter poverty—indeed, squalor—of the circumstances of Christ's birth did not arise by accident. Here was surely a divine demonstration that the Son of God wished to be identified from the beginning in a special sense with those in greatest need and weakness.

But the birth, for all its obscurity, was not to pass altogether unnoticed. Some shepherds were tending their flocks nearby—although according to one theory they would have driven their sheep into one of the caves and been keeping watch outside against wolves or robbers. "And an angel of the Lord appeared to them, and the glory of the Lord shone around them." The shepherds were terrified; it was not the first or last time that an angel bringing good news produced this reaction. He now told them to put aside their fears. He brought them "good news of a great joy." This, he added significantly, should be for all people. "For to you," he continued, "is born this day in the city of David a Savior, who is Christ the Lord." This would be "a sign": They would find the baby wrapped in swaddling clothes lying in a manger. Suddenly the angel was surrounded by a "multitude of the heavenly host." They praised God continuously and cried aloud, "Glory to God in the highest and on earth peace among men with whom he is pleased." Without delay the shepherds hurried off, and they found Mary and Joseph and the baby Jesus exactly as the angel had told them. They returned spreading the news far and wide and praising God. All to whom they spoke wondered.

Certain ceremonies had then to be performed in a devout Jewish family. After eight days came circumcision, the symbol of the covenant between God and Abraham and his descend-

ants. The child now officially received the name of Jesus. After
that came purification. A woman was considered unclean after
the birth of a child until she was purified in the temple and an
offering made: a lamb, if it could be afforded, or, as here in the
case of a poor family, a pair of turtledoves (or pigeons). Jesus
came with his parents to be formally presented and was
greeted unforgettably by a devout old man called Simeon,
who had been assured that he would not die until he had seen
the promised Messiah. Taking Jesus in his arms, he proclaimed
the *Nunc Dimittis* employed so widely in Christian churches
at nightfall and at the hour of death:

> Lord, now lettest thou thy servant depart in peace,
> according to thy word;
> for mine eyes have seen thy salvation
> which thou hast prepared in the presence of all peoples,
> a light of revelation to the Gentiles,
> and for glory to thy people Israel.

What he said to Mary was perhaps even more significant:

Behold, this child is set for the fall and rising of many in Israel,
and for a sign that is spoken against
(and a sword will pierce through your own soul also)
that thoughts out of many hearts may be revealed.

Here, more clearly than in the original salutation of Mary by
the angel, is set forth the idea of the Messiah as a suffering
servant of humanity tormented by a hostile world rather than
a triumphant earthly king, and of Mary as a mother not only
of joys but also of sorrows. Anna, a woman as old and devout
as Simeon, also testified to Christ and spoke of him "to all who
were looking for the redemption of Jerusalem." These ceremonies completed, Mary and Joseph returned to Bethlehem,
though this time it would seem to some more or less adequate
lodging.

*   *   *

Within a short time the birth became a major problem for the government. "Wise men from the east came to Jerusalem, saying, 'Where is he who has been born king of the Jews? For we have seen his star in the East, and have come to worship him.'" Herod was far too intelligent not to be gravely alarmed. The threat to his own position needed no underlining. He immediately assembled all the chief priests and scribes and asked them where Christ was to be born. They answered him unambiguously, "In Bethlehem of Judea." Herod thought of what seemed a shrewd maneuver. He blandly sent the wise men off to Bethlehem with the instructions, "Go and search diligently for the child, and when you have found him bring me word, that I too may come and worship him." The wise men took him at his word, though if they were as wise as we suppose, they had their reservations.

"And lo! the star which they had seen in the east went before them, till it came to rest over the place where the child was." They went in, found Jesus with his mother Mary, and fell down and worshiped him. They offered him their gifts: gold, frankincense, and myrrh. Gold is the traditional symbol for a king, frankincense for a god, myrrh for the bitterness of the man predestined to death. Whether or not they had already seen through Herod, an angel warned them against him, so they made their way to their own country by another route.

Joseph received a similar and even more vital warning in a dream. Herod, he was told, was seeking to destroy the young child. He must set off at once with his family to Egypt. This he did just in time. Herod, outwitted by the wise men, was determined to achieve his sinister purpose and guarantee his own security. He calculated that if he killed all the babies in or around Bethlehem he could hardly fail to do this. He would be bound to liquidate, incidentally, a future aspirant to his throne. He embarked therefore on his notorious massacre of the innocents—that is, of all the babies under two in Bethlehem and the surrounding area. The number may not have been large, perhaps twenty-five in Bethlehem itself, but the fiendishness of the operation has given it an indestructible niche in the history of horrors.

Herod died soon after, the worst of all his many bad deeds accomplished. Yet once more an angel appeared to Joseph in a dream, this time to tell him that the coast was clear and it was safe to return. For reasons that have not come down to us, Joseph's inclination was to settle in Judea. But at that time Herod's son Archelaus was still ruling there, and he was no improvement on his father. So Joseph withdrew with his family to Galilee, to the village of Nazareth, where they had been living previously. We are told by St. Matthew that in this way he fulfilled the prophecy, "He shall be called a Nazarene." But no one, it seems, can trace the prophecy in question.

＊　＊　＊

For twenty years now we lose sight of Jesus, with the exception of one brief glimpse to be mentioned shortly. One thing at least is certain: He lived the life of the poor. Today a church marks the supposed site of the house where Jesus was brought up. It is largely subterranean, hollowed out of the soft local limestone. There is a crude stairway where a child could climb up and down, now richly decorated with mosaics.

Jesus would almost certainly have received the same education as all the young Jews of his time. It revolved round the synagogue and provided him with a thorough knowledge of the law. Whether he attended more advanced academies than the village school, none can say. Assumptions will vary as to the extent to which he needed or benefited from human instruction. He was capable at an early age of arguing with experts on the law on equal terms. We can all have our own ideas as to how he acquired his knowledge. Only once is the veil drawn aside.

Every year his parents went to Jerusalem at the feast of the Passover. When he was twelve a strange thing happened. His parents were returning from Jerusalem and did not at first realize that Jesus was missing. They thought he must be somewhere among the considerable party of friends and relatives. But it turned out not to be so. They returned, no doubt in great anxiety, to Jerusalem. It was not until three days had passed that they came upon him in the temple, "sitting among the teachers, listening to them and asking them questions." It was quite common for children to sit with the students in the temple; they were sometimes allowed to ask questions. But all who heard Jesus were amazed at his understanding and his answers. Not surprisingly, his parents were astonished. His mother, in spite of her awareness of his divine nature and mission, could not help saying to him reproachfully: "Son, why have you treated us so? Behold, your father and I have been looking for you anxiously." He replied, surprised in his turn: "How is it that you sought me? Did you not know that I must be in my Father's house?"

His parents, we are told, did not understand what he meant, though Mary must have had more than an inkling and "kept all these things in her heart." What they could understand and appreciate was that he did go back with them to Nazareth, and he was "obedient to them." The episode in the temple, with its sudden self-assertiveness and hint of self-revelation, stands on its own. We are told that from now on he "increased in wisdom and stature and in favor with God and man." Can we then attribute his demonstration in the temple partly to immaturity? Did he himself decide that it had been somewhat premature?

3

"He must increase, but I must decrease"

The recorded story of Jesus is only resumed when he is a man of thirty-three, the day he sought and received baptism from John the Baptist. But before beginning his mission, Jesus decided on a period of solitude.

Jebel Qarantal is the mountain traditionally associated with the retreat of Jesus to a "desert place apart," to be tempted by the Devil. It is quite close to Jericho, but has been described as one of the most forbidding places in the Judean desert. It was a terrain not unsuited for the satanic aggression that now followed.

Jesus was seeking silence and solitude for the purpose of spiritual preparation. We do not think of him deliberately courting temptation. But what he did do deliberately was fast for forty days so that, when temptation arose, he would be physically at his most vulnerable.

The gospels describe the temptations as personal interventions by the Devil. Some Christians see the struggle rather as the resistance of Christ to the concentrated powers of evil, which he would have to encounter if he was to share genuinely in the human experience. The personalized language of the gospels may be accepted symbolically or otherwise.

We are sometimes told that the temptations were primarily aimed at diverting him from his divine purpose, but in resisting them he stood for all of us who encounter the same temptations at one moment or another in normal existence.

Christ rejected three temptations: to turn stones into bread, to throw himself down from the temple, and to accept control of the world in return for worshiping the Devil. No human being of any sensitivity can fail to realize that here were presented the ultimate challenges that confronted him in his human existence. But inevitably the question arises: "How much of a genuine temptation did these allurements offer to Christ?" They are dismissed in the gospel accounts so curtly, so contemptuously, that one is left wondering whether, in any ordinary sense, Christ was tempted at all. And yet one must believe that if he did become like us in all things, his temptations must have been at least as painful as ours. He would not in any real sense have been a human being if he had not undergone the human experience of withstanding temptation. We are told in the epistle to the Hebrews: "He has been through every trial fashioned as we are, only sinless." He won, it is true, a total victory, but it was anything but a phony war.

The first temptation relied on his inevitable craving for food after forty days and nights of fasting and on his extremely vulnerable condition. "If you are the Son of God," said the Devil, "command these stones to become loaves of bread." Jesus answered: "It is written, 'man shall not live by bread alone, but by every word that proceeds from the mouth of God.'" It is no doubt permissible to see here his rejection of all sins of the flesh, but it is surely just as possible to point out to non-Christians, who consider Christians to be obsessed with sex, that sex is noticeably *not* referred to explicitly. Various explanations can be offered: On one understanding of sexual excesses, they are not due so much to physical yearning as to a psychological need for self-glorification. In any case, the fact of the nonreference provokes reflection.

The next two temptations are aimed at the cravings for power and for public applause. These headings do not exhaust the temptations to which most ambitious men are subject. Today we draw a further distinction between power and influence. If you have power, you can order that such and such a thing must be done. If you only have influence, you have to persuade someone or some authority to do it for you. In each case the pleasure of recognition is never far absent.

Jesus was first offered all the kingdoms of the world; then he was invited to throw himself from the pinnacle of the temple, with the assurance that he would come to no harm. The replies he provided—"You shall worship the Lord your God, and him only shall you serve" and "You shall not tempt the Lord your God"—were interwoven. Nothing but worship of God can overcome deification of self. To tempt God comes close to seeking to suppress one's higher nature in the corruption of oneself and others.

* * *

Jesus came from the mountain and returned to the banks of the Jordan. The time had come to collect around himself a band of faithful, carefully selected disciples. A few weeks earlier John the Baptist had pointed out Jesus, as Jesus passed by, to two young men: John, later the evangelist, and Andrew, who had traveled from Galilee to listen to the Baptist. "Behold, the Lamb of God," he had said. Now Jesus found the pair following him. "What do you seek?" he asked them. They were fascinated and showed it. "Rabbi," which means Master, they asked him, "where are you staying?" "Come and see," said Jesus. They went and saw where he was living and stayed with him all that day. It was the beginning of their lives' commitment. Simon, Andrew's brother, happened not to be with them when they met Jesus. They left Jesus saying, "We have found the Messiah"—one more significant indication of the general state of expectancy. Simon was not slow to return with them to Jesus, nor Jesus to pick him out for a special destiny. "So you are Simon," he said to him, "the son of John? You shall be called Cephas," which means a stone or a rock. Simon was from now on earmarked for an exceptional vocation. But for some time yet its nature was to remain mysterious.

Jesus and his three new disciples were soon on their way back to Galilee. We find them next at Bethsaida, home of Andrew and Simon, henceforth called Peter. There Jesus came across Philip and straightaway said to him: "Follow me." Philip responded without question. Philip was soon announcing fervently: "We have found him of whom Moses in the law and also the prophets wrote, Jesus of Nazareth, the son of Joseph." His hearers were not overwhelmingly impressed. Nazareth was to them a rather obscure village across the mountains. "Can anything good come out of Nazareth?" asked one of them, Nathaniel, skeptically. Philip replied in the words Jesus had used to John and Andrew: "Come and see."

Philip and Nathaniel approached Jesus, who took Nathaniel aback by remarking: "Before Philip called you, when you were under the fig tree, I saw you." Nathaniel was astonished at being spotted in this way from afar. His skepticism disappeared. He went to the other extreme and cried out: "Rabbi! You are the Son of God. You are the King of Israel." Jesus replied that he had not yet begun to see the marvels in store. In due course he would see the heavens open, "and the angels of God ascending and descending upon the Son of Man." Already the theological titles are multiplying: the Messiah, the King of Israel, the Son of God, the Son of Man.

And now came the first of the miracles: "The first, the kind miracle," as Aloysha called it in *The Brothers Karamazov*. Jesus, with his disciples, possibly all five of them, repaired to Cana in Galilee, perhaps sixteen miles from Bethsaida, to attend a wedding feast, where his mother was also present. At least two villages, Kefr Kenna and Kirbet Qana, compete today for the honor of providing the exact site. At some point the wine failed. Mary said to Jesus, a little helplessly it might seem, but with instinctive confidence: "They have no wine." Jesus replied in words that are often translated: 'O woman, what have you to do with me? My hour has not yet come." The words in English sound harsh and unfilial, but "woman" was in fact a courteous style of address and was also used by Jesus in speaking to his mother from the cross. The rest of the sentence, however, still seems a little strange, in view of what immediately followed. Can it be that he was reluctant to embark quite so soon on the tragic destiny?

Mary, at any rate, was sure that her son would not let them down. She turned to the servants: "Do whatever he tells you." There were six stone jars close by, available for the Jewish rites of purification. Jesus said to the servants: "Fill the jars with water," and when they did so: "Now draw some out, and take it to the steward of the feast." They did as they were told. When the steward of the feast had tasted the wine, he made the classic comment to the bridegroom: "Every man serves the good wine first; and when men have drunk freely, then the poor wine. But you have kept the good wine until now." The bridegroom in the circumstances may not have relished the intended compliment, but he was at least rescued from an awkward predicament and no doubt thought it best to keep silent.

❋ ❋ ❋

We are now in March A.D. 28. A good deal was to happen before Jesus was ready to begin his public ministry in Galilee.

At this point he returned to Jerusalem, where huge crowds would come together for the Passover, not only from Palestine but also from surrounding settlements. Here Jesus was to reveal himself in a light that must have astonished his followers.

The temple conceived and embarked on by the lamentable Herod the Great was magnificent, if still incomplete. There were four courts rising higher and higher—the court of the Gentiles, the court of the (Jewish) women, the court of the

Israelites and, finally, the court of the priests. In the outer court, Gentiles changed money from "unclean" Greek and Roman coins to the Jewish coins necessary for religious Jews; here, too, animals were sold by the priests for sacrifice. This court presented a noisy and wordly spectacle, which might well have offended a devout Jew.

On arrival, Jesus found a typical scene: people selling oxen, sheep, and pigeons, and money changers at their business. He made a whip of cords, and, without any ado, "drove them all, with the sheep and oxen, out of the temple; and he poured out the coins of the money changers and overturned their tables. And he told those who sold the pigeons: 'Take these things away; you shall not make my Father's house a house of trade.'"

The crowd was clearly impressed by this extraordinary young man, who could cow and disperse a multitude by his personal authority. As usual, they looked for religious credentials. "What sign have you," they asked him, "to show us for doing this?" Jesus told them that if they destroyed the temple, in three days he would raise it up. The Jews took this literally, and were naturally puzzled. It had taken them forty-six years to build the temple. Was he really saying that he could raise it up in three days? "But he spoke of the temple of his body." It was not until after his resurrection that any of this was understood by his disciples.

Word was now going around about him, though he was not yet engaged in what might be called a public ministry. The news stirred the interest of Nicodemus, "a man of the Pharisees, a ruler of the Jews," in fact a member of the Sanhedrin. Some of us will always find Nicodemus a specially attractive figure. He appears three times in the gospel story, always timidly, and yet in a sympathetic light.

He came to Jesus under cover of darkness and said to him: "Rabbi, we know that you are a teacher come from God; for no one can do these signs that you do, unless God was with him." Jesus replied at something of a tangent. "Truly, truly, I say to you, unless one is born anew, he cannot see the kingdom of God." Nicodemus was honestly puzzled, but he was a genuine seeker after truth and persisted. How could a man be born again when he was quite old? Was he to enter into his mother's womb once more? Jesus tried to explain that he was talking in a deeper sense altogether. "Unless one is born of water and the Spirit, he cannot enter the kingdom of God." Nicodemus continued to admit himself mystified. Christ suggested that a teacher of Israel should understand these things.

Christ went on to deliver to this solitary nocturnal visitor what has been called a summary of his entire teaching. Some of it must have seemed unintelligible at the time. "No one," he said, "has ascended into heaven, but he who descended from heaven, the Son of Man. And as Moses lifted up the serpent in the wilderness, so must the Son of Man be lifted up." But there was nothing ambiguous in the words that followed: "For God so loved the world that he gave his only Son, that whoever believes in him should not perish but have eternal life. For God sent the Son into the world, not to condemn the world, but that the world might be saved through him."

Jesus and his disciples returned to that part of Judea where John was still baptizing and teaching. For a while the two groups may have appeared to be competing, but John soon put a stop to any such possibility. His disciples not unnaturally looked to him for guidance. Who was this newcomer whom John himself had baptized? What were his claims in relation to those of John? John replied in perhaps the most touching utterance ever delivered by a great man superseded by a greater: "You yourselves bear me witness, that I said, I am not the Christ, but I have been sent before him. He who has the bride is the bridegroom; the friend of the bridegroom, who stands and hears him, rejoices greatly at the bridegroom's voice; therefore this joy of mine is now full. He must increase, but I must decrease."

John's last words bore an even more poignant meaning than was probably intended. Herod the tetrarch had done many evil things and now appropriated Herodias, his brother's wife. John did not hesitate to rebuke him and found himself confined in the grim fortress of Macherus.

* * *

Jesus and his disciples now set off once more for Galilee. The time for his public ministry had come. If he had conducted it in Judea, a premature confrontation would seem to have been inevitable.

His party followed the hill road rather than the Jordan Valley on their three-day journey to Galilee. Their way led them through Samaria, whose population had for many years been antagonistic toward the Jews. When the northern kingdom had been overrun by the Assyrians, Samaria had been repopulated with every sort of immigrant, bringing a varied stock of idolatry. Jews did not travel through Samaria if they could avoid doing so.

On the second day the party had traveled about fifty miles and were approaching Shechem, famous among other reasons as the burial place of Joseph. It was about the sixth hour—in other words, about midday. They would have been hot, dusty, and in need of refreshment. The disciples went off to the town to buy food. Jesus sat down by what had been known for centuries as "Jacob's well." A woman of Samaria came to draw water. Jesus said to her: "Give me a drink."

The woman started off with crude, if legitimate, curiosity. How was it that this Jewish stranger asked her, a Samaritan, for a drink? For, in St. John's words, the Jews have no dealings with Samaritans. Jesus began to help her realize that she was dealing with someone quite out of the ordinary: "If you knew . . . who it is that is saying to you, 'Give me a drink,' you would have asked him, and he would have given you living water." Her curiosity was further aroused. How could he draw living water from a deep well when he had nothing to draw with? Was he setting himself up as superior to "our father Jacob, who gave us the well, and drank from it himself and his sons, and his cattle"?

Jesus told her in effect that that was exactly what he was doing. "Every one who drinks of this water will thirst again, but whoever drinks of the water that I shall give him will never thirst; the water that I shall give him will become in him a spring of water welling up to eternal life."

The woman was now completely won over. She begged him to give her this mysterious water, that she might not thirst any more, nor have to come to draw from the well. Jesus might have left the matter there, but instead carried it much farther. He asked the woman to call her husband. When she replied that she had no husband, he told her that she was perfectly right. She had had five husbands and her present partner was no husband of hers. Now the woman really was astonished. Clearly he possessed supernatural powers. He was obviously a prophet.

But she continued the argument, and not unintelligently. "Our fathers worshiped on this mountain; and you say that in Jerusalem is the place where men ought to worship." How could both things be true, she implied, if God was rational. Now Jesus came right out into the open. It was true that at present there was a distinction between Samaritans and Jews. "You worship what you do not know; we worship what we know, for salvation is from the Jews." That, however, was no more than a preliminary truth. The hour was coming when "neither on this mountain nor in Jerusalem will you worship the Father." The worship of God was something much more profound than any geographical accident. "But the hour is coming, and now is, when the true worshipers will worship the Father in spirit and truth."

He had said not long before to Nicodemus: "Unless one is born of water and the Spirit, he cannot enter the kingdom of God." Now he spelled out in a few unequivocal words the explanation: "God is spirit, and those who worship him must worship in spirit and truth." The woman, slightly dazed by now, could only murmur that she knew that when the Messiah came he would show them all things. Jesus, speaking more plainly on this point than previously or for some time to come, told her: "I who speak to you am he." Then the disciples arrived, surprised to find him talking with a woman but not venturing a comment. The woman, happily excited, forgot her water jar and went off to the city, telling everyone, "Come, see a man who told me all that I ever did." Many of them came to the well to meet Jesus and, while not giving proper credit to the woman, finished by announcing, "we know that this is indeed the Savior of the world."

4
The Miracle Worker

Now began the systematic ministry in Galilee, which covered half of Jesus' public life; it apparently lasted from May A.D. 28 to the autumn of the following year. In that period he appears to have paid one short visit to Jerusalem and two other visits outside the province. One was to Tyre and Sidon and the other to Caesarea Philippi, also north of Galilee, where the tetrarch Herod Philip II had his capital. For something like five hundred days Jesus was traveling around, mostly on foot, though it is argued that he must sometimes have been mounted to complete the distances in the time. His audiences would have been engaged in fishing and husbandry and incidental crafts.

"There are also many other things," says St. John at the end of his gospel, "which Jesus did; were every one of them to be written, I suppose that the world itself could not contain the books that would be written." We only possess a small portion of Jesus' words and deeds, handed down to us through the evangelists, without any strict regard for chronology. For example, one cannot place exactly the following episode in his home village, Nazareth. Jesus entered the synagogue on the Sabbath; this was "his custom," as St. Luke points out. On being given the book of the prophet Isaiah to read from, Jesus found the place where it was written:

The Spirit of the Lord is upon me,
because he has anointed me to preach good news to the poor.
He has sent me to proclaim release to the captives
and recovering of sight to the blind,
to set at liberty those who are oppressed,
to proclaim the acceptable year of the Lord.

He sat down and, as so often, "the eyes of all in the synagogue were fixed on him," that mysterious fascination once again at work. They were not going to like what they heard. "Today," he told them, "this scripture has been fulfilled in your hearing." From that moment they seemed to realize, dimly perhaps, but disquietingly, that he was making some novel and far-reaching claim on his own behalf. This they could not easily swallow from Joseph's son. Drawing on the familiar stories of Elijah and Elisha, he drove home the lesson: "No prophet is acceptable in his own country." This was really too much for them. They rose in their wrath and would have thrust him over the brow of the hill. But "passing through the midst of them," he left them. When it came to the point, no one at this stage of his career could pluck up courage to lay hands on him.

He "went down to Capernaum." This journey to the shores of the Lake of Gennesareth, also referred to as Lake Tiberias or the Sea of Galilee, might have taken him ten hours on foot. At that time the countryside surrounding the Sea of Galilee was fertile and green. Vines and olive trees grew on the hills, and the shores were covered with fruit trees. Capernaum itself was essentially a Jewish city, not Hellenistic in culture like the neighboring towns. It was here that he had begun the combination of teaching and healing that was to carry his name far and wide.

We know little of his teaching on this occasion, except that he told his audience that the kingdom of God was at hand. They must repent "and believe in the gospel." What is notable is that "they were astonished at his teaching, for he taught them as one who had authority, and not as the scribes." Here, as so often in the times to come, he was to demonstrate his indefinable personal authority. As was freely said at the time, "never did any man teach as this man." This widespread reaction does not of course prove him divine, but one would have expected no less from the appearance of divinity.

No doubt his personal authority was much strengthened by the abundant miracles of healing. In the synagogue there was a man "with an unclean spirit." In the gospel account the unclean spirit cries out, "What have you to do with us, Jesus of Nazareth? . . . I know who you are, the Holy One of God." Jesus rebuked him, saying, "be silent and come out of him." The unclean spirit, "convulsing him and crying with a loud voice, came out of him."

Many Christians today, including incidentally the present writer, will accept absolutely the fact of this and similar miraculous cures. Some of them will translate both the diagnosis and the remedy into the language of mental illness. But the gospel version is how it struck onlookers at the time and was remembered afterward. There is no reason to doubt the profound impression that resulted.

After Simon's mother-in-law is described almost incidentally as being cured of a fever (most of the apostles, like Simon himself, appear to have been married men), there comes one of the most famous of all the scenes in the gospels.

"Now when the sun was setting, all those who had any that were sick with various diseases brought them to him; and he laid his hands on every one of them and healed them. And demons also came out of many, crying, 'You are the Son of God!'" However we translate the last sentence into our own language, it is clear that physical and mental illness were placed on precisely the same footing by Jesus Christ. That idea has never been followed up since, the mentally sick being treated with contempt in Christian and non-Christian societies alike for many centuries. In recent years there are at last signs of an improvement, with modern psychiatry helping to introduce in this field the original Christian values.

Jesus had no intention of unduly localizing his endeavors. "Let us go on," he said, "to the next towns, that I may preach there also; for that is why I came out." And he went, accompanied by Simon and a faithful few. "And he went about all Galilee, teaching in their synagogues and preaching the gospel of the kingdom and healing every disease and every infirmity among the people." Once again, the preaching and the healing are part of the same operation. Soon they were bringing him "all the sick, those afflicted with various diseases and pains, demoniacs, epileptics and paralytics." Without hesitation he healed them. But we are still told little of what the "gospel of the kingdom" meant to this mass of simple enthusiasts. One has a suspicion that it did not mean much. For the moment the magnetism and the miracles were sufficient.

Jesus was now a celebrity. His fame had spread beyond Galilee. Great crowds, the gospel tells us, followed him, not only from Galilee, but "from the Decapolis and Jerusalem and Judea and beyond the Jordan." Perhaps his activities had already been noted with interest by the Jewish leaders: the strange, well-attested tales coming out of Galilee of miraculous healings; the fracas in the temple, and Jesus' pointed lack of reverence for the religious establishment. But so far Jesus was probably regarded more as a wonder than a threat. The time was yet to come when the authorities would decide that he was too dangerous to live.

Three particular cures occurred in this halcyon period: a leper, a paralytic, and a man with a withered hand. In each case the actual healing is disposed of almost curtly, but a significant addendum is emphasized.

"And a leper came to him beseeching him, and kneeling said to him, 'If you will, you can make me clean.'" Jesus was "moved with pity." He stretched out his hand and touched the leper and said the simple words: "I will; be clean." The leper was cured at once. Jesus told him to show himself to the priests and to offer for his cleansing what Moses had commanded. But he was not to say anything to the general public—an instruction immediately disregarded. Jesus was anxious to avoid unnecessary publicity at this stage, but to demonstrate at the same time his strict adherence to Jewish law and custom.

The paralytic has come down to us as the man let down on a bed or "pallet" through the roof by his friends to avoid the throng. But the procedure adopted by Jesus on this occasion is at least as striking as the miraculous performance. He began by saying to the paralyzed man: "My son, your sins are forgiven." Not unexpectedly, this produced an immediately hostile reaction among the scribes, although they did not apparently express it openly. "Why," they said to themselves, "does this man speak thus? It is blasphemy! Who can forgive sins but God alone?" Jesus read their minds and, it may well be, their faces. He said to them, in effect: "I suppose you think that anyone could say to anyone else 'your sins are forgiven' without any supernatural endowment. But if you have any doubts whether any real spiritual power lies behind my words, I can soon set them at rest." To the paralytic he said: "Take up your pallet and go home," which the paralytic had no difficulty in doing. One cannot believe that in any case the paralytic would have been left with his sins forgiven but his physical affliction uncured. No doubt in all Christ's miracles of healing the predominant motive was compassion. But the occasion was often taken, as here, to demonstrate his supernatural power to the skeptics.

Finally, the man with the withered hand. Jesus was teaching in a synagogue on the Sabbath day when a man with this affliction came up to him. Healing on the Sabbath was strictly forbidden by the law, and Christ had shown a careful respect for the law up to that moment. The Pharisees awaited the outcome with bated breath. Jesus, as so often, went onto the offensive. He got the man to come and stand in front of the company and challenged the Pharisees directly to choose between legalism and humanity in the actual case in front of them. "Is it lawful on the Sabbath to do good or to do harm, to save life or to destroy it?" he demanded of them. Put that way, the question admitted of only one answer, as he knew and they knew. They maintained an embarrassed silence. To the man he said: "Stretch out your hand." He did so, and was healed forthwith. Jesus had won a popular victory, but the worsted legalists were left muttering darkly to themselves and beginning to plan his physical destruction. Meanwhile, a great multitude from Galilee followed him as he "withdrew to the sea." But the crowds came also from Judea and Jerusalem and Idumea and from beyond the Jordon, and from around Tyre and Sidon. All who had diseases "pressed upon him to touch them." He told his disciples to have a boat ready for him, mainly, it would seem, to avoid being physically crushed.

* * *

Sometime in June of this year, A.D. 28, he chose the remainder of his twelve apostles: Peter, Andrew, James, John, Philip, and Nathaniel (Bartholomew) had been picked already. But it seems that they, like the newcomers, now received a formal authority. Jesus deliberately spent the night in solitary prayer before selecting this small band, who he was one day going to refer to as his friends.

Peter was bold and sanguine, but overexcitable and liable to intense discouragement. He was a fisherman, but he owned a house, a boat, and all the gear necessary for his work. According to one view, he employed as day laborers the fisherman Zebedee and his family. Peter knew what he was saying when he said to Jesus: "Behold, we have left all and followed you." Was there anything in his character that led him to be selected as the leader of the apostles and the head of the infant Church? His impulsive nature had at once a credit and a debit side. Everyone must select in Peter the qualities that appeal to him most. To me it will always be a kind of total responsiveness. When he failed, he failed utterly. But no one was ever more capable of picking himself up again and going farther and farther, regardless of everything except the divine inspiration and grace.

Andrew, Peter's brother, was public-spirited and courageous, but considering that he was one of the "big four," remains a somewhat obscure figure. We shall come across him occasionally, but never very excitingly. He is famous for the cross on which he was martyred. According to tradition, it was in the shape of the letter X, which is also a Greek letter, the initial letter of the word for "Christ." When Andrew's time came, he greeted his cross with the unmistakable words *"Salve Crux."* They are a sufficient memorial.

James and John, sons of Zebedee, were surnamed by Christ "Boanerges," sons of thunder. The gospels give us two examples of their impetuousness and presumptuousness in youth. On one occasion they asked Jesus to call down fire from heaven on an unwelcoming Samaritan city. On another occasion they asked if they could sit, one at his right hand, one at his left, when he was in his glory. But such weaknesses were transcended. Somewhere about Eastertime, in the year A.D. 42, James was the first of all the apostles to drink of the cup of martyrdom.

As we read and reread the gospel of John and his epistles and the Book of Revelations, we find it hard to equate their author with the qualities just attributed to the sons of Zebedee. He was a mere boy or adolescent in the lifetime of Jesus. When he died in Ephesus he was something like a hundred years old, and no one after Jesus himself has ever embodied more completely the religion of love.

Philip has been described as "possessed of a dull and dry personality." Yet it was Philip who made the most moving request in the whole of the gospels: "Lord, show us the Father." In apocryphal writings he is repeatedly depicted as in battle with a serpent or a dragon, but in fact we know little of his works or his death. We can be sure that whatever he did was thoroughly practical. At the time of the feeding of the five thousand, it was to Philip that Jesus put the question "Whence shall we buy bread that these may eat?" He was not looking for an answer; he was just paying a graceful compliment to the business expert.

Matthew has a double name—Matthew Levi. Socially he was unlike and above the other apostles. He was probably older and certainly better educated. His role of tax collector or publican no doubt aroused initial suspicion. We cannot tell how far he overcame this. He kept a close and far from kindly eye on Judas. Of the four evangelists, he alone noted how many pieces of silver Judas was paid for betraying his master. Matthew's gospel never loses sight of Jesus' fulfillment of the historic prophecies. But it would be wrong to treat it as a purely Jewish document. The great agnostic Renan called it "the most important book of universal history."

Thomas is usually referred to as a skeptic or doubter. It would be truer to describe him as pessimistic or melancholy. We shall find him making the boldest affirmation of faith of any of the apostles, after displaying the most hesitancy. In the multiple legends that grew up around his name, it is difficult to separate fact from fiction. It is seriously argued that at one time he made his way to China; we cannot be quite sure, but it is at least highly probable that he did great pastoral work in India.

James the Less, Jude, Thaddeus, and Simon (not Peter) were all related to Jesus, though certainly not his brothers. Of these, Jude and James wrote epistles—the letters to the faithful. In the epistle of James, we have the ever-famous definition "Religion that is pure and undefiled before God and the Father is this: to visit orphans and widows in their affliction, and to keep oneself unstained from the world." It was almost certainly this James who, after the Resurrection, became head of the Church in Jerusalem.

There was one other apostle, Judas Iscariot, of whom for many centuries it was unthinkable to say anything not entirely pejorative. Today, when we regard it as closer to the spirit of Jesus to adopt the formulation "to understand all is to forgive all," we are most of us anxious to enter, however inadequately, into his motives. It is difficult to believe that it was avarice that led him into his supreme act of betrayal. He sold his master for much less than the customary price of a slave. But it would be going to the other extreme to find any motive of idealism at work. Jesus must have seen much good in him when he selected him as one of his intimate followers. But we are assured by the evangelists that quite soon he recognized that Judas had a devil. The most charitable explanation is that Judas had crude nationalist ideas for Jesus and became infuriated when he found that Jesus had no intention whatever of fulfilling them. Perhaps the simplest and truest thing would be to say that Judas, a man of average morality, came to resent the perfect man in Jesus so emotionally that he could not bear his company any longer.

But let us never forget that Judas repented. After the condemnation of Jesus, Judas went to the high priest and tried to hand back the blood money, saying without qualification: "I have sinned in betraying innocent blood." They treated him with contempt and he went and hanged himself. People sometimes ask about well-known criminals: "Do they show any remorse?" Judas answered that question at least. A little earlier, at the time of Jesus' arrest, he said to Judas: "Friend, why are you here?" We can believe that Jesus died even for Judas.

*   *   *

It was during this stage of Christ's ministry in Galilee that he preached the Sermon on the Mount. "Seeing the crowds, he went up on the mountain, and when he sat down his disciples came to him." Then he began to preach.

It is still not certain where this sermon was delivered. Some say at Tabgha, twelve miles north of Tiberias and about two and a half from Capernaum, where there is what has been called a "graceful hill," close to the lake. A great gathering could easily have been accommodated there. But it is felt by others that the site of the sermon must have been some wild and solitary place. There is considerable support for Quorum or Karn Hattin (Horns of Hattin), a high plateau between two sharply conical hills. Personally, I am ready to fall in behind Daniel-Rops when he writes: "It must have been in some place like this, some lonely sunlit place of wide horizons, rocks and shrubs, and not in the Rembrandtesque setting of classical porticos and ruins that the immortal words were spoken."

The Sermon on the Mount has been said to contain the essence of Christianity. Many non-Christians will say they accept the Christian ethic, mentioning the Sermon on the Mount specifically. Certainly, anyone who lived up to its teaching would be well on the way to sanctity. Whether all the sayings contained in Matthew 5–7 were in fact delivered in a single speech need not bother us unduly. What matters is their blinding truth and undying influence.

However, to appreciate the underlying theology of the gospels one must go far beyond the sermon. There is the whole of St. John to start with. Nor do we find in the Sermon on the Mount what Our Lord described as the first two commandments: "You shall love the Lord your God with all your heart, and with all your soul, and with all your strength, and with all your mind; and your neighbor as yourself." And the two most distinctive features of Christian ethics, humility and forgiveness, are no more than adumbrated here. All this can be said without disputing its claim to be regarded as the greatest sermon in world history.

A great crowd pressed around Jesus, many of them yearning for his healing touch, as he began to utter the eight famous beatitudes. Blessed are the poor in spirit, those who mourn, the meek, those who hunger and thirst for righteousness; blessed are the merciful, the pure in heart, the peacemakers, those who are persecuted for righteousness' sake. Can we or can we not regard this as a revolutionary code of ethics? Personally, I think we can.

Jesus affirmed, "Think not that I have come to abolish the law and the prophets; I have come not to abolish them but to fulfill them." They had been told not to kill; Jesus said that it was sinful to be angry. They had been told not to commit adultery; he said that it was sinful to lust after a woman. They had been told to give a divorced wife a certificate; he said that divorce itself was wrong. It was no longer sufficient to avoid false swearing; Jesus told them not to swear at all.

The most famous modifications of all lie in the instructions: "You have heard that it was said, 'An eye for an eye and a tooth for a tooth.' But I say to you, Do not resist one who is evil. . . . You have heard that it was said, 'You shall love your neighbor and hate your enemy.' But I say to you, Love your enemies, and pray for those who persecute you."

The next few sentences carry us deeper and deeper. It is not enough to love those who love us, or to extend a cordial welcome to our family and friends. Such things are the common practice of mankind generally, including pagans. The real test is whether we can bring ourselves, force ourselves, to love those whom it is natural to dislike or even hate—it may be for their hostility or contempt toward us, or for bringing us into ridicule. In the eyes of the world Jesus does not spell this out at this point precisely. Softness and gentleness may be regarded as "bad business" and inimical to successful ambition. But they are essential to Christian conduct.

Such a transformation of instinctive attitudes is barely possible without a fundamental, far-reaching belief in God the loving Father. Each of us is infinitely precious in his sight. That is equally true of ourselves and of those who lack our beliefs and behave in what seems to us a deplorable manner. The Father, we are told here, makes the sun rise on the evil and the good and sends down rain alike on the just and on the unjust, or those who seem to us to deserve those descriptions.

Nowhere in the gospels are we called on for a more strenuous battle at the very center of our souls.

In the following section, he sets out for the first time the Lord's Prayer, which is too familiar to require quotation but in which we ask for our daily bread, for rescue from evil, for forgiveness of our own sins, and for the power to forgive those of others.

The historian of Jewish thought is entitled to point out how much Jesus owed, in a human sense, to the old law. But whatever may be said of later Jewish teaching, it is beyond dispute that in the Sermon on the Mount Jesus went far beyond all previous ethical reformers. One cannot disagree with Bishop Sheen when he writes: "He was going beyond the Mosaic law, Buddah with his Eightfold Way, Confucius with his rules for being a gentleman, Aristotle with his natural happiness, 'the broadness of the Hindus' and, for that matter, the humanitarians of our time."

Jesus was introducing values of a different order, not the values of success, the values to put the practitioner at the top of the most respectable obituary column, but the only values that would mean something to the Father in heaven. It was, in a vital sense, a code of perfectionism, and indeed it culminated in a call to perfection. "You, therefore, must be perfect, as your heavenly Father is perfect." His code is never likely to be lived up to by imperfect human beings, but it remains a standard, higher than any previously held out to us, capable of endless study and deeper comprehension, and in its underlying principles, binding forever.

5
Speaking in Riddles

Jesus came down from the mountain and the flow of miracles was resumed, many of them works of healing.

A Roman centurion came to him with a pathetic story of a servant lying paralyzed at home, in deep distress. Jesus responded without hesitation. "I will come and heal him." But the centurion would not hear of it. In a memorable combination of faith and humility, he used the immortal words: "Lord, I am not worthy to have you come under my roof; but only say the word, and my servant will be healed." He himself was "a man under authority." He could say to a subordinate "Go!" and he went. No one knew better than he did the meaning of discipline and obedience. A word from Jesus was enough. Jesus, we are told, "marveled." One of the strongest tributes, it would seem, that he ever paid to a human being. "Not even in Israel have I found such faith." He issued one of his firmest warnings that the Jews, if they persisted in their lack of faith, would be supplanted by the Gentiles. The latter would come from all over the world "and sit at table with Abraham, Isaac, and Jacob," while "the sons of the kingdom will be thrown into the outer darkness." To the centurion he said: "Go; be it done for you as you have believed." It transpired that the centurion's servant was healed at that very moment.

Jesus now showed that he had power over nature as well as men. He and his disciples were in a boat on the Sea of Galilee. While he was sleeping peacefully a mighty storm arose. The disciples woke him in terror: "Teacher," they cried, "do you not care if we perish?" He "rebuked the wind and said to the sea; 'Peace, be still!'" The wind ceased and a great calm followed. He did not neglect to point the moral. "Why are you afraid," he said, "have you no faith?" For the time being at least, their faith was strengthened, as they said to one another: "Who then is this, that even wind and sea obey him?"

Perhaps the most controversial episode in the story of Jesus' miracles occurred in the country of the Gadarenes. "There met him out of the tombs a man with an unclean spirit, who lived among the tombs." He seemed a hopeless case. No one could hold him down. He had often been bound with fetters and chains, but he tore the chains apart and broke the fetters in pieces. He wandered about the tombs and on the mountain, crying out and bruising himself with stones.

Jesus addressed the unclean spirit directly, ordering him to "come out of the man." The unclean spirit replied: "What have you to do with me, Jesus, Son of the Most High God?" He begged Jesus not to torment him. Jesus was not ready to leave it at that. "What is your name?" he asked. "My name is Legion, for we are many." And a strange request followed. He asked that the spirits should be allowed to enter a herd of swine that were feeding on the hillside. Jesus gave permission. The unclean spirits entered the swine and the latter, about two thousand of them, rushed down the steep bank into the sea and were drowned.

Unlike most of the miracles, this one met with a poor reception. The local inhabitants begged Jesus to depart from the neighborhood. In the circumstances, that is comprehensible enough. Harder to understand is why a large number of swine should have been required to perish as part of the therapeutic operation. That must always remain a question without a dogmatic answer. But we must remember that while compassion was the driving force in the miracles of Jesus, they were also demonstrations of his divine power.

❀ ❀ ❀

There are three occasions in the gospels when Jesus brought to life someone who was dead. On one of these occasions a great crowd had gathered about Jesus while he was beside the sea. One of the rulers of the synagogue called Jairus came to him, fell at his feet, and begged him piteously: "My little daughter is at the point of death. Come and lay your hands on her, so that she may be made well, and live." Jesus went along with him, followed and pressed hard by a great crowd.

Among them there was a woman who had had a "flow of blood for twelve years." We are told that she had suffered much under many physicians. She had spent all her money and was no better. In fact, she was getting worse. She had heard much about Jesus and saw in him her last chance. She did not even venture to ask him to perform a miracle. In any case, it might not have been physically possible for her to secure his attention. She said to herself: "If I touch even his garments, I shall be made well." And she touched his clothes. The hemorrhage ceased immediately. She knew instinctively that she was cured. Jesus also was immediately aware that he had performed a miracle; that power, or, in some translations, virtue, had gone out from him. He swung around and asked the crowd: "Who touched my garments?" The disciples gaped at him a little hopelessly. In view of the numbers jostling him, how could anyone possibly answer this question? But the woman, in a mixture of pride and fearfulness, came forward, fell down before him, and told him what had happened. He said to her with his unfailing gentleness: "Daughter, your faith has made you well; go in peace, and be healed of your disease."

But now a messenger arrived from Jairus' house with gloomy

tidings. "Your daughter is dead. Why trouble the Teacher any further?" But Jesus would not have been affected by such a report. To the ruler of the synagogue he said: "Do not fear, only believe." He himself set off again, accompanied only by Peter, James, and John, James' brother. When they reached Jairus' house, he found a "tumult"; people were weeping and wailing loudly. Jesus addressed them in a manner that at first made no impression. "Why do you make a tumult and weep?" They simply laughed in his face. "But he put them all outside, and took the child's father and mother and those who were with him, and went in where the child was. Taking her by the hand he said to her, *Talitha cumi*,' which means, 'Little girl, I say to you arise.' And immediately the girl got up and walked." Those present were "overcome with amazement."

* * *

By now Jesus had done too much and said too much not to be viewed with indignation and alarm by the religious establishment. The disputes with the Pharisees and scribes were multiplying. Jesus had broken the conventional rules, exhibiting powers that they could not possibly accept were of divine origin. When he cast a demon out of a dumb man, the people marveled, but some said that he cast out demons by Beelzebub, the prince of demons. His retort implied that if this were indeed true, there would be a division among the followers of Satan that would bring them to destruction: If Satan is divided against himself, how will his kingdom stand? The Jewish leaders were committing the appalling sin of attributing the Holy Spirit to the Devil. "Every sin and blasphemy will be forgiven men, but the blasphemy against the Spirit will not be forgiven."

There came a stage during the Galilee ministry when Jesus abandoned his simple, direct method of teaching and sometimes, though by no means always, took to speaking in parables.

The word "parable" comes from the Greek *parabilein*, meaning a comparison. The Hebrew word *maschail* is vaguer and much more complex. It seems that this adornment of speech was much favored by Jews as a telling form of argument. We need not therefore be surprised that it was adopted by Jesus. It is true that when asked by the apostles why he spoke in parables he replied: "To you it has been given to know the secrets of the kingdom of heaven, but to them it has not been given." This statement, however, should not perhaps be taken too literally. His doctrine here, as in the case of his messiah-ship, was so intellectually and spiritually revolutionary that it could only be gradually, if at all, understood by his immediate hearers. His first task was to kindle an enormous eagerness for the truth, whether among his disciples or others in the years to come. Who can doubt that this purpose was in fact achieved by these "comparisons," which have retained their direct appeal throughout the centuries?

Some of the most famous of the parables were delivered after Jesus had left Galilee. Eight parables, all relating to the kingdom of heaven, were spoken in Galilee and are contained in a single chapter of the gospels, Matthew 13. He compares it in turn with the seed sown by the sower in various kinds of terrain, with the field where an enemy comes to sow tares by night, and with the grain of mustard seed, the smallest of all seeds, which grows into a tree so that the birds of the air come and make nests in its branches. He also compares it to the leaven that a woman hides in three measures of meal, the treasure hidden in a field, the single pearl of great value, the net thrown into the sea that gathers fish of every kind, and the householder's treasure that contains what is new, but also what is old. It will be noted that at least four of the eight para-bles relate to grain or bread. Here, as always, he drew his ex-amples from the basic requirements of human beings in all ages.

Taking the eight parables in Matthew 13 together, Jesus is concerned to illustrate the growth of the kingdom of God from small spiritual beginnings, but never to let us forget that

at every point of our progress the choice must be made between good and evil. Of all these parables, the story of the
sower is the most famous. Some of the seeds fall by the wayside
and are devoured by the birds; others on rocky ground, where
they become scorched by the sun; others among thorns, which
grow up and choke them; others on good soil, where they pro-
duce a plentiful harvest. Though it is hard to pick out a single
lesson to be learned here, these four examples cover so much
of human nature that not even the most arid sociologist could
deny their relevance to our condition.

Some months had passed since Jesus began to preach in Galilee. As he went about the cities and villages, preaching and
healing, he had compassion on the crowds, because they were
harassed and helpless, "like sheep without a shepherd." No
doubt this thought stirred his next action. "The harvest," he
said to his disciples, "is plentiful, but the laborers are few; pray
therefore the Lord of the harvest to send out laborers into his
harvest." And he proceeded to do this. He called together
his twelve disciples and gave them power to heal diseases,
whether physical or mental. But he was still giving first priority
to the Jews. "Go nowhere among the Gentiles, and enter no
town of the Samaritans, but go rather to the lost sheep of the
house of Israel." As they went they were to preach saying:
"The kingdom of heaven is at hand," and at the same time to
heal the sick of every description.

He laid on them a strict ascetic rule. They had received no
pay and they were to render their services for nothing. Their
way of life was to be simple. "Take no gold, nor silver, . . . no
bag for your journey, nor two tunics, nor sandals, . . . for the
laborer deserves his food." They would have to expect some
harrowing experiences. "Behold, I send you out as sheep in
the midst of wolves; so be wise as serpents and innocent as
doves." They would be delivered up to hostile authorities and
flogged in the synagogues. But there was no need for them to
be anxious as to how to speak or act in even the most parlous

situations, for "it is not you who speak, but the spirit of your Father speaking through you." They could go forward in the sublime assurance that "he who receives you receives me."

It would seem that this mission of the apostles lasted about two months, early in A.D. 29, but the guidance permeated the rest of their lives, and may fairly be held to represent the original title deeds of the Christian churches.

✿ ✿ ✿

The Pharisees as a class were hostile to Jesus, but one of them, Simon, asked Jesus to eat with him, a point mentioned without comment by St. Luke. It was, presumably, not a unique nor yet a common occurrence. "And behold, a woman of the city, who was a sinner, when she learned that he was at table in the Pharisee's house, brought an alabaster flask of ointment, and standing behind him at his feet, weeping, she began to wet his feet with her tears, and wiped them with the hair of her head, and kissed his feet, and anointed them with ointment. . . ."

Simon was shocked and disillusioned. If Jesus had been a genuine prophet, he said to himself, he would easily have spotted that this woman was a "sinner." He would no doubt have rejected her attentions. Jesus read his mind without difficulty. Simon, he said, let me tell you a story and ask you a question. "A certain creditor had two debtors; one owed five hundred denarii, and the other fifty. When they could not pay he forgave them both. Now which of them will love him more?" Simon, driven into a corner, replied: "The one, I suppose, to whom he forgave more." Jesus told him that he was quite right. Then he turned around to the woman and said to Simon: "Do you see this woman? I entered your house, you gave me no water for my feet, but she has wet my feet with tears and wiped them with her hair." Simon had given him no kiss but she had not ceased to kiss his feet. Simon had not anointed his head with oil. But she had anointed his feet with ointment. A painful silence no doubt ensued before Jesus drove home the moral. "Therefore I tell you," he said, "her sins, which are many, are forgiven, for she loved much; but he who is for-given little, loves little."

The gospel version chosen is deliberately ambiguous at the crucial point. Which came first? The forgiveness of the sins or the selfless and dedicated love? One must not presume to try to settle the argument dogmatically, but a version in which "many sins are forgiven her for she loved much" will always be the one with the widest appeal.

To the woman he said: "Your sins are forgiven." The fellow guests were startled. "Who is this," they asked one another, "who even forgives sins?" Jesus' assurance was unshaken and absolute. He said to the woman, "Your faith has saved you; go in peace."

This incident is only recorded by St. Luke, although the three other evangelists record another later at Bethany, near Jerusalem.

* * *

Jesus proceeded through the cities and villages "preaching and bringing the good news of the kingdom of God." He was ac-companied by the twelve apostles and also by "some women who had been healed of evil spirits and infirmities: Mary, called Magdalene, from whom seven demons had gone out, . . . and many others." These women "provided for them out of their means." We shall meet Mary Magdalene again at the foot of the cross, beside the tomb of Jesus, and in his first en-counter with a human being after his resurrection. But perhaps we have met her already? Was she the sinner who anointed him in the house of Simon the Pharisee? Again, looking for-ward, should we also identify her with Mary of Bethany, the sister of Martha and Lazarus, with whom Jesus stayed more than once in the last few months of his life? This question of one woman, two women, or three women has produced more books than one, including the learned, imaginative, but highly speculative volume by Father R. L. Bruckberger.

He is convinced that Mary Magdalene came of a great Sadducean family, with a country house on the shores of Lake Gennesareth in Galilee and a town residence at the gates of Jerusalem. "Young Mary had been brought up in Greek style; she was Greek to her fingertips. She had a dancing master who came from either Ephesus or Eleusis. She had him read aloud from the symposium Diotima's speech on Free Love as the best means of attaining wisdom, or had him talk to her about Phryne, the fashionable Greek courtesan." On the concrete points at issue, he is crystal clear: Mary of Bethany is beyond doubt the same woman as the sinner. Mary Magdalene is most probably also this same woman. It is on this latter hypothesis that his absorbing narrative is based; though he is the first to admit that there has always been, and continues to be, total disagreement on this subject among Christian authorities. I must record my opinion that all the evidence on the face of the gospels points to there having been three women. If it were otherwise, the evangelists would surely have said so.

* * *

We last heard of John the Baptist when he was imprisoned by Herod Antipas in the grim and lonely fortress of Macherus for denouncing Herod for taking possession of Herodias, his brother Philip I's wife. Fairly soon afterward, somewhere in the summer of A.D. 28, John sent a message from his cell to Jesus. He put this surprising question: "Are you he who is to come, or shall we look for another?" Surprising, because after all John had baptized him and had himself seen the Holy Spirit descending on him in the form of a dove. Had John lost his confidence in Jesus in the psychological confusion not uncommon in prison? One cannot say. Jesus in any case provided a convincing answer. "Go," he said to the messengers, "and tell John what you have seen and heard: The blind receive their sight, the lame walk, lepers are cleansed, and the deaf hear, the dead are raised up, the poor have the gospel preached to them." Jesus had testified more than once to John's superb qualities and lofty mission. "A prophet . . . and more than a prophet," he now called him; he said that no one born of a woman was his superior. We must take it that John's doubts were dispelled.

But John's jailer, Herod—"that fox," as Jesus called him on one occasion—continued to play a crafty waiting game with John, impressed, it would seem, by some mysterious power in John, regarding him as a potential menace but uncertain of the right course of action to adopt in his own interest. It may well be that left to himself he would have continued to spare him, but his new consort Herodias, wife of his brother Philip I, was biding her time and not for a moment abandoning the idea of revenge for John's denouncement of the adultery between Herod Antipas and herself. There came a point when she could at last hold royal court at Macherus, where Herod stopped for a while, probably on his way back from Mesopotamia. John was now physically within her grasp.

She found her instrument in her daughter Salome, aged perhaps thirteen or fourteen, and, as it is always assumed, full of sexual appeal. Salome dánced and pleased Herod and those who sat with him. Herod fell a complete victim to her charms. "Ask for whatever you wish," he said to her, "and I will grant it." And he swore that "whatever you ask me, I will give you, even half of my kingdom." Surely no king ever promised a dancing girl more than that. Salome, for all we know, was innocent up to this point of any special malice. However, she dutifully asked her mother what her prize should be. Herodias, who had planned the operation carefully, had no doubt whatever about the answer. She told Salome to go straight back and ask for the head of John the Baptist, which Salome promptly did.

At this point we feel a kind of sympathy for Herod, who was well and truly trapped. We are told that he was "exceedingly sorry." He had grown fond of John and by no means excluded the possibility that his claims were valid, but his strange idea of honor—or was it prestige—prevailed. "Because of his oath" he fell in with Salome's request, and an executioner was dispatched to the prison to behead John and bring his head on a charger to Salome.

Salome, still the obedient daughter, handed the head to her mother, who displayed it in triumph, we can assume, in front of Herod and the uproarious company. Even so, Herodias was not quite satiated. Transported with joy and triumph, according to St. Jerome she pierced the tongue of John the Baptist with a stiletto: that same tongue that had originally denounced her.

When John's disciples heard of it they came and took his body and reverently laid it in a tomb. And when the news reached Jesus in his turn, he used words to his disciples that showed that he fully comprehended their sorrow and at the same time underlined his own. "Come away by yourselves," he said to them, "to a lonely place, and rest a while." And they went away with Jesus in a boat to a lonely place, but Jesus' admirers spotted them and were not going to be given the slip. They made their way around the lake on foot and arrived there first.

When Jesus came ashore he saw "a great throng." He took pity on them "because they were like sheep without a shepherd." It was a situation to which he could never fail to respond. He taught them without knowing or caring how the time was passing. At last the disciples felt bound to intervene. "This is a lonely place," they pointed out, "and the hour is now late; send them away, to go into the country and the villages about and buy themselves something to eat." Jesus, testing them or teasing them, replied: "You give them something to eat." They asked him whether he was serious. Did he expect them to go and buy 200 denarii worth of bread (a denarii was a day's wage for a laborer). He asked them what food they had got and was told five loaves and two fishes. Then he commanded them "all to sit down by companies on the green grass." Taking the five loaves and the two fishes, he looked up to heaven and blessed and broke the loaves and gave them to the disciples to set before the people, and he divided the two fishes in the same way. We are told that all ate and were satisfied. Five basketfuls of fragments were collected, and five thousand men shared in the meal.

It was a sensational, euphoric moment, but the sequence of events was far from ended. He got the disciples to row back across the lake while he himself, as on so many other occasions, withdrew to the mountain to pray. St. John puts it most clearly. "Perceiving then that they were about to come and take him by force to make him king, Jesus withdrew again to the mountain by himself."

While he prayed, the disciples found themselves in serious difficulties: Their boat was "beaten by the waves, for the wind was against them." In the fourth watch of the night (i.e., between 3 A.M. and 6 A.M.), Jesus came to them walking on the sea and, not for the first or last time, they were terrified at any appearance of their master that deviated from the normal. "It is a ghost!" they cried out in fear. But immediately he reassured them. "Take heart, it is I," he said, "have no fear." Peter, impetuously to the fore as always, spoke out excitedly: "Lord, if it is you, bid me come to you on the water." Jesus said the single word, "Come." Peter set off boldly enough, but "when he saw the wind, he was afraid, and beginning to sink he cried out, 'Lord save me.'" Jesus reached out, took him by the hand, and escorted him to the boat, saying in mild reproach, "O man of little faith, why did you doubt?" The wind dropped. Everyone relaxed, and for the moment at least their reverence was unqualified. "Truly," they said to Jesus, "you are the Son of God."

 · When they all reached land, Jesus was immediately recognized. Word went around the district. All who were sick were brought to him from far and wide, and begged to touch just the fringes of his garment, and "as many who touched it were made well." In a human sense this was the apex of his worldy existence. But St. John makes us realize that Jesus was determined not to win a single supporter on a false prospectus. He did not at this time actually institute the rite of Holy Com-

munion—that was reserved for the Last Supper. But philosoph-
ically and theologically he now prepared the way for the sacra-
ment. On the day after the miracle of the loaves and fishes,
Jesus felt bound to explain that most of the enthusiasm toward
him was for the wrong reasons. "You seek me," he said,
". . . because you ate your fill of the loaves. Do not labor for
the food that perishes, but for the food that endures to eternal
life, which the Son of Man will give to you." For God the
Father had set his seal on him. Again and again, he insistently
claimed their belief in his unique power to satisfy their spiritual
needs.

They kept coming back, however, to their request for a
"sign." This manufacture of bread, apparently out of nothing,
was all very well, but after all, Moses had done as well or better. He had given their ancestors their "bread from heaven" in
the wilderness. Jesus told them gently but firmly that "my
Father gives you the true bread from heaven." No other bread
but this could bring life to the world. His audience was by now
won over or confirmed in the hopes they reposed in him.
"Lord," they said, "give us this bread always."

He now judged the moment right for one of the boldest of
all his sayings. "I am the bread of life; he who comes to me
shall not hunger, and he who believes in me shall never
thirst." But this was going too far for many of them. They
began to "murmur" because he said that he was the bread that
came down from heaven. Once again, and perhaps not very
surprisingly, they asked themselves who this young person
thought he was. They knew his "father" Joseph and his mother
perfectly well. What was all this nonsense about his coming
down from heaven?

He spoke still more plainly. "No one," he said, "can come to
me unless the Father who sent me draws him," and he added
for good measure: "and I will raise him up on the last day."
And then, finally and unmistakably: "He who eats my flesh
and drinks my blood abides in me, and I in him."

It is clear that he had deliberately set out, at this moment of popular enthusiasm, to enforce the truth. Many of his own disciples said: "This is a hard saying; who can listen to it?" And after further clarification a considerable number "drew back and no longer went about with him." Jesus felt it encumbent on him to test the belief of his inner core, the twelve apostles. "Do you also wish to go away?" Simon on this occasion at least responded perfectly. "Lord," he said, "to whom shall we go? You have the words of eternal life; and we have believed, and have come to know, that you are the Holy One of God." Jesus' answer reads somewhat cryptically. "Did I not choose you, the twelve, and one of you is a devil?" We know now, as the evangelists knew, that the remark referred to Judas. There is no evidence that the apostles paid any attention to it. They seem to have acquired a remarkable talent for passing over what they could not understand.

6
The Messiah

At about this point, a change came over the style of Jesus' ministry. He abandoned or played down his public appeal to the masses and concentrated on enlightening his disciples and preparing them for the great ordeal to come. We are not told this in so many words in the gospels. The change, however (summer A.D. 29), roughly coincides with his movement away from Galilee itself. For most of the summer he would seem to have been traveling around the country to the north of the province; we hear of him in Tyre and Sidon and at a very celebrated moment in Caesarea Philippi. Various explanations can be offered for this double shift of emphasis.

The Jews, or at any rate some of their leaders, were now seeking to kill him. He would face, and even court death in due course, but not till his mission was accomplished and the appointed time had come. Had the masses themselves rejected him? Had he lost his hold on the people? This, again, would be at most part of the truth. On one occasion at least during this period he reappeared beside the Sea of Galilee. He went up "on the mountain, and sat down there. And great crowds came to him, bringing with them the lame, the maimed, the blind, the dumb, and many others, and they put them at his feet, and he healed them." When they saw yet again the miracles of healing "the throng wondered . . . and they glorified the God of Israel." The enthusiasm was as unrestrained as ever. There followed the second miracle of the loaves and fishes. This time four thousand men, women, and children were amply fed with seven loaves and "a few small fishes." This time seven baskets were filled with the leftover broken pieces.

Taking this episode and the other data into account, it would seem that at this point that Christ felt himself not so much rejected as misunderstood. The people simply could not understand that his role was spiritual. After the first loaves and fishes miracle, St. John in particular leaves one with the impression that public opinion reached its highest point of fervor. People cried out, as we have seen, "This is indeed the prophet who is to come into the world." It was then that Jesus, realizing that they were going to take him by force and make him king, withdrew alone onto the mountain. The very next day, in his famous description of himself as "the bread of life," he set out in his usual enigmatic way to correct the misunderstanding; to explain that the kingdom he stood for was spiritual, not material. After this, as we have seen, there was considerable drawing back. We must bear all this in mind when we come in a moment to his acceptance of the title of Messiah.

One of the most touching of all the miraculous cures occurred at this time. As Jesus toured through the district of Tyre and Sidon, a Canaanite woman from that part of the world approached him and cried: "Have mercy on me, O Lord, Son of David; my daughter is severely possessed by a demon." Jesus said nothing. The disciples found her a nuisance and begged him to send her away. It seemed, for a moment—a horrifying thought if it had been true—that he was actually complying with their request. He said to her: "I was sent only to the lost sheep of the house of Israel." But, as he well knew, she was not the kind of mother to be disposed of so easily. She came and knelt before him, saying, "Lord, help me." Again he adopted an attitude of seeming brutality. "It is not fair," he said, "to take the children's bread and throw it to the dogs." She made one of the great answers of history. "Yes, Lord, yet even the dogs eat the crumbs that fall from their master's table." Jesus answered her, surely with joy in his heart, "O woman, great is your faith! Be it done for you as you desire." And her daughter was healed instantly.

When they arrived at Caesarea Philippi, probably in July, he seemed to feel that a new stage had been reached and that the disciples were ready for a fuller and clearer revelation. He put to them the question "Who do men say that the Son of Man is?" They replied that some said he was John the Baptist, others Elijah, and others Jeremiah or one of the prophets. All are answers that strike us curiously today, particularly as Jesus had actually been baptized by John the Baptist. But now came the crucial question: "But who do you say that I am?" Simon Peter was again first to speak up: "You are the Christ, the Son of the living God." Jesus answered him: "Blessed are you, Simon Barjona." Flesh and blood had not revealed this to him, but "my Father who is in heaven."

Here, then, Jesus formally accepted and welcomed the title of Christ or Messiah. But almost equally significant is what he said a few moments later: "He strictly charged the disciples to tell no one that he was the Christ."

There has been endless argument as to why Jesus was so slow to reveal himself as the Messiah in this unmistakable fashion. One must not forget that he had already revealed himself as the Messiah to the Samaritan woman at the well. No doubt those with eyes to see and ears to hear could have extracted a similar acknowledgment of his role from various other utterances. It seems reasonable, however, to treat the question-and-answer sequence that he deliberately initiated at Caesarea Philippi as something novel and full of significance.

* * *

Apart from the statement to the Samaritan woman, there are only two instances in which Jesus accepted the title Messiah. The first occasion was the one at Caesarea Philippi; the second, to which we shall come later, was when the high priest asked him at his trial, "Are you the Messiah?" Authorities disagree as to whether or not Jesus accepted the title unambiguously, as I think, but it is certain that he did not wish the claim to be widely known. Why this reluctance? It seems to me that one explanation common among scholars is largely convincing. Jesus was carrying out in some ways the historic function expected of the Messiah, but in other ways he was going so far beyond it spiritually as in fact to refute it.

In the popular mind the Messiah was associated with the political and military role of the Son of David. To play that part was the last thing Jesus desired. Yet the role of the Messiah was one in a spiritual sense, which he could not possibly repudiate. He was in something of a dilemma. If he simply accepted the title of Messiah, his true function would be totally misunderstood and fatally blurred. Yet he could not repudiate that title without repudiating all that was best in the Old Testament, and his historic function in carrying it onto a new plane. It seems correct, therefore, to conclude that the title Messiah was always an embarrassment to Jesus. The discussion with his disciples at Caesarea Philippi was a step in their education. The time had come when it was safe to explain these matters, partially at least, to them. But certainly not to blazon the title all over Galilee and Judea, where it would certainly have been misunderstood in a fashion most damaging to his true message.

He also had a special and historic message for Peter. "And I tell you," he said, "you are Peter, and on this rock I will build my church, and the powers of death (or, as some say, hell) shall not prevail against it. I will give you the keys of the kingdom of heaven, and whatever you bind on earth shall be bound in heaven, and whatever you loose on earth shall be loosed in heaven." The Roman Catholic Church, as is well known, finds in these promises the strength of its own title deeds, recognizing St. Peter as its first Pope.

Two important propositions had already been expounded: that Jesus was the Messiah (though this revelation was not yet to go beyond the apostles) and that Peter was to be the rock on which the Church was to be founded. From that time Jesus began to lay bare a still more profound connection between his moral teaching and his theology.

Jesus began to explain to his disciples "that he must go to Jerusalem and suffer many things from the elders and chief priests and scribes, and be killed, and on the third day be raised." The strength of Peter's reaction to this intimation is astonishing, and Jesus' reaction in his turn at first seems hardly less so. "Peter took him and began to rebuke him, saying: 'God forbid, Lord! This shall never happen to you.'" Jesus turned on him with crushing force: "Get behind me, Satan! You are a hindrance to me; for you are not on the side of God but of men." What led Peter to issue the only rebuke to the Master on the part of the disciples? And whence came the extraordinary vehemence of the reprimand? One can be sure that it was not the result of wounded dignity.

Even Peter had not yet begun to understand what kind of messiahship Jesus had in mind when he accepted this historic title. Peter's messiah—and we have no reason to suppose that his comrades were more enlightened—was a victorious kind, sweeping away all the forces of evil and elevating Israel in final triumph. A messiah who was defeated and put to death was totally unlike this leader that he and the others were yearning for. It was not for this kind of humiliated figure that he and the others had forsaken everything to follow Jesus. It was as though Winston Churchill in the middle of World War II had suddenly revealed to his colleagues that he would in due course be defeated and put to death by Hitler. It is true that Jesus stated at the same time that he would rise again, but perhaps that point hardly registered in their horrified minds.

The extreme words used by Jesus can no doubt be attributed to more than one cause. Bitter disappointment, in the first place. Could even Peter, the leader he had so carefully selected, not begin to obtain some inkling of what Jesus really represented? And was Jesus here resisting an internal temptation? From the record of the temptations in the wilderness, we can assume that the possibility of using his divine powers to win the kind of victory his admirers expected was a real allurement. And it was presumably present throughout his life up to the moment he died on the cross. In castigating Peter was he not denouncing and suppressing the frailty, and what one can only call the ambition, that were inherent in his human nature?

But this was not all, as he made plain very soon afterward. He told his disciples: "If any man would come after me, let him deny himself and take up his cross and follow me. For whoever would save his life will lose it and whoever loses his life for my sake will find it. For what will it profit a man, if he gains the whole world and forfeits his life?" Here in two or three sentences is the Christian doctrine of suffering. It is reproduced and expanded elsewhere, especially in regard to redemptive suffering, but basically it is contained in this passage. Jesus is not only breaking the news that he himself must undergo unlimited suffering to achieve spiritual victory. He is revealing that spiritual or moral victory is impossible for anyone without suffering. That it is the law of life for everyone in search of perfection. It may take the form of external persecution or of internal agony and self-conflict. But suffering in one form or another is inevitable for anyone who seeks to follow Christ.

A few days later—six in the gospels, eight according to our modern reckoning—the disciples were given, for the only time, a glimpse of Jesus' supernatural role. An argument still continues as to whether this occurred on Mount Tabor or Mount Hermon. The two are joined in Psalm 89, which tells us that "Tabor and Hermon joyously praise thy name." Tradition from the fourth century designated Mount Tabor, a modest hill 600 feet high in the middle of Galilee, in spite of the fact that at the time of Christ it was an inhabited area. Mount Hermon, 2,800 feet high, always referred to as the foremost mountain of Israel, is close to Caesarea Philippi, where Jesus had been just previously. It seems a much stronger candidate.

The evangelists were very positive and unambiguous about the fact of the Transfiguration. Jesus took Peter, James, and his brother John, the evangelist, and brought them apart onto "a high mountain" (the phrase suggests strongly it was Hermon). For a long time Jesus was sunk in prayer. The disciples, as was to happen on a still more testing occasion, fell fast asleep. When they awoke, an extraordinary sight met their eyes. Jesus was transfigured before them, "his face shone like the sun, and his garments became white as light. And behold, there appeared to them Moses and Elijah, talking with him." Peter rushed into the breach in his most enthusiastic vein. "Lord, it is well that we are here. If you wish I will make three booths [sometimes translated "tabernacles"] here, one for you, and one for Moses, and one for Elijah." What reception such a suggestion would have received we can only guess. For he was still speaking when a bright cloud enveloped them and a voice from the cloud said: "This is my beloved Son, with whom I am well pleased." The disciples were awestruck, and threw themselves on their faces. But Jesus came and touched them, saying: "Rise, and have no fear." When they lifted up their eyes, there was only Jesus there.

Once again Jesus enjoined on them the utmost secrecy. "Tell no one the vision, until the Son of Man is raised from the dead." The disciples were still puzzled. They asked him why the scribes said Elijah would have to return to earth before the arrival of the Messiah. "Elijah," he said enigmatically, "has already come, and they did not know him, but did to him whatever they pleased. So also the Son of Man will suffer at their hands." For once the disciples understood a cryptic allusion. They realized that when he talked of Elijah he was referring to John the Baptist.

The Transfiguration was obviously no causal development. It was a metamorphosis that gave St. Peter an irrefutable vision, an overwhelming testimony. We must bear in mind that in these crucial days Jesus was implanting in the disciples the revolutionary consciousness that the messianic kingdom was something quite unexpected, and that he must suffer and die to achieve it. The Transfiguration, then, was designed to inspire the apostles with a "certitude of their faith." In this it may be said to have been ultimately successful. But that success was to come much later, after the Crucifixion and Resurrection had clarified in their minds the true significance of what was said and seen and done on the mountain.

At least one notable miracle occurred when they came down from the mountain. A man came up to Jesus, knelt before him, and said: "Lord, have mercy on my son, for he is an epileptic and he suffers terribly; for often he falls into the fire and often into the water." The disciples had been quite unable to heal him. Jesus did not conceal his censure: "O faithless and perverse generation," he cried, "how long am I to be with you? . . . Bring him here to me." The boy was brought to him, the demon was cast out, and an instant cure effected. The disciples asked Jesus in genuine puzzlement: "Why could we not cast it out?" He told them it was because of their weakness of faith. "If you have faith as a grain of mustard seed, you will say to this mountain, 'Move from here to there,' and it will move; and nothing will be impossible to you." Words of great encouragement, one would think. But he labored once again the harsh realities in the near future. "The Son of Man," he said, "is to be delivered into the hands of men, and they will kill him, and he will be raised on the third day." We are told that the disciples were greatly distressed. They were beginning to understand the tragedy, but not yet the triumph, in store for them.

* * *

The time was coming when Jesus would leave Galilee never to return. One more great discourse was to be delivered there, probably at or near Capernaum. It stands with the Sermon on the Mount and the loving addresses recorded in St. John 13–18 as the most systematic statement of the ethics of Jesus. One could spend a lifetime meditating on the description of this address in Matthew 18, and still find new meaning. The various themes are so interwoven that it is almost impossible to pick them out in order. Yet the attempt must be made.

When Jesus is preaching forgiveness, there is a moment when he urges the victim of somebody else's sin to "tell it to the church." But he then breaks off to deliver a different kind of pronouncement altogether. "Truly," he said, "I say to you, whatever you bind on earth shall be bound in heaven, and whatever you loose on earth shall be loosed in heaven." He had used exactly the same words to Peter when he gave him his special mandate at Caesarea Philippi. He now provided an additional indication of how the Holy Spirit would operate. "If two of you agree on earth about anything they ask, it will be done for them by my Father in heaven." The worldwide Roman Catholic Church and the smallest nonconformist sect can extract their own measure of authenticity from these various statements. For the moment, we are concerned with facts and not deductions.

But this is not the main message of the address. We said earlier, in discussing the Sermon on the Mount, that the two most distinctive features of Christian ethics, humility and forgiveness, are barely touched on there. They are spelled out clearly in Matthew 18, forgiveness at much greater length than humility. On humility, St. Mark memorably summarizes Jesus' teaching: "And he sat down and called the twelve; and he said to them, 'If any one would be first, he must be last of all and servant to all.'" (Compare St. Luke to the same effect.) No one ever came as near to exemplifying that truth as Jesus Christ in his life and death.

Let us now take a look at the words actually used by Jesus

on this occasion at Capernaum. "Who is the greatest in the kingdom of heaven?" he asked. "And calling to him a child, he put him in the midst of them, and said, 'Truly, I say to you, unless you turn and become like children, you will never enter the kingdom of heaven. Whoever humbles himself like this child, he is the greatest in the kingdom of heaven. Whoever receives one such child in my name receives me.'"

What do those few sentences really amount to? We are told unmistakably that we must become like children if we wish to enter the kingdom of heaven. But what aspect of children are we to emulate? Children are physically helpless. In that sense they are in need of help, like the old and the sick. They are also conscious of their dependence on their parents, and lack the pride that is the supreme curse of adults. Again they are innocent, or relatively so. The shades of the prison house, morally speaking, have not begun to close in. In all these ways we must learn to copy children. But that is not the whole of the teaching. "Whoever receives one such child, in my name receives me; but whoever causes one of these little ones who believe in me to sin, it would be better for him to have a great millstone fastened around his neck and to be drowned in the depth of the sea." Jesus goes on to say that we must on no account despise these little ones. For "in heaven their angels always behold the face of my Father who is in heaven."

His thought now becomes very complex. If a man has a hundred sheep and one of them goes astray, does he not leave the ninety-nine on the mountains, and go in search of the one that went astray? If he finds it, he rejoices over it more than over the ninety-nine that never went astray. The next statement is the surprising one. "So it is not the will of my Father who is in heaven that one of these little ones should perish." This seems a surprising conclusion to this part of the argument, because nobody is suggesting, Jesus least of all, that these little ones have gone astray. As so often in the gospels, two ideas are developed together, in a manner that is anathema to modern academics.

The first fifteen verses of St. Matthew bring out, somewhat obliquely, the meaning of humility—but also overwhelmingly the emphasis that Jesus laid on sheer human need, whether due to our own fault or someone else's, or no one's fault at all. His tenderness toward children is one glorious example of his universal sympathy for all who need help, and the more desperate the need, the more urgent his compassion. In that sense the lost sheep and the little children are on the same footing. But so, as he goes on to explain imperatively, are sinners.

Peter came up to him and said to him: "Lord, how often shall my brother sin against me, and I forgive him? As many as seven times?" Jesus said to him: "I do not say to you seven times, but seventy times seven," and he went on to illustrate the point with a powerful anecdote, which finished with the warning that his heavenly father would not forgive anyone who does not forgive his brother from his heart. Many draw unyielding inspiration from the double exhortation to "hate the sin and love the sinner." One cannot find a scriptural authority for it, but no nonscriptural utterance seems closer to the spirit of Christ.

The discourse we are discussing is firm enough for anyone in its denunciation of sin. "And if your hand or your foot causes you to sin, cut it off and throw it away; it is better for you to enter life maimed or lame than with two hands or two feet to be thrown into the eternal fire." It does not set out to lay down a penal philosophy, or to solve in detail the intractable problem of finding a Christian and humane form of punishment, a problem to which each generation struggles to provide the best solution in its power. But it makes it absolutely clear that resentment and bitterness, as opposed to forgiveness, are utterly un-Christian, and that the sinner is just as much in need of help as the most helpless and innocent of victims.

7

"The man whom they seek to kill"

In the autumn, Jesus left Galilee, never to return. It was surely inevitable that he should consummate his life's work in Jerusalem and perish, if he had to perish, there, at the heart and center of the faith. He had visited the city briefly during the summer and effected there the cure of a paralyzed man in a manner that aroused general attention. From then on he made three major appearances in Jerusalem. At the Feast of Tabernacles in October A.D. 28, at the Feast of Dedication of the temple in December of the same year and, finally, when he entered it on Palm Sunday, at the beginning of A.D. 30. In between he traveled and lodged in various parts of Judea, a barren, rocky land in contrast to the fertile, fortunate Galilee. Early in A.D. 30 he spent some time in Perea.

The Feast of Tabernacles was one of the most solemn of all the Jewish feasts. Five days earlier the Day of Atonement would have been celebrated, when the symbolic scapegoat, charged with the sins of Israel, was driven out into the desert. The Feast of Tabernacles itself was an occasion of profound joy and gratitude. In recollection of their days of wandering in the desert and the tents they had lived in then, each Jew had to leave his house and for eight days live in a tent or hut made with branches. The whole city and the surrounding area, including the balconies of houses, were covered with structures that qualified under these headings. The whole scene was one of Jewish piety at its happiest.

For reasons that can only be guessed at, Jesus did not go up to the feast publicly, as his allies had suggested to him, but in private. As always, he took immense trouble over the timing of his operations. Certainly he was in no mood to conceal himself for long from his potential friends or enemies. The general public in Jerusalem, no doubt aware of his Galilean exploits and recalling his summer miracle in the capital city, were eagerly discussing his personality and probable actions. "He is a good man," said some, but others took the view that he was leading the people astray. For fear of the Jews, no one spoke openly of him—the discussions went on in lowered voices. They had not long to wait for his next move.

About the middle of the feast, Jesus went boldly into the temple and taught. The Jews (the same rather ambiguous phrase) marveled, saying: "How is it that this man has learning when he has never studied?" In the most unambiguous term Jesus insisted on the divine source of his message, and he carried the war into their camp.

Circumcision was permitted on the Sabbath so that the law of Moses might be kept. Why did the Jews object to his healing a man's "whole body" on the Sabbath? For, according to Jesus, they were seeking to kill him because of the miracle of healing he had performed on his earlier visit. His opponents said that he must be demented: No one was trying to kill him; yet there seemed a general impression that on this point he was quite right. "Is not this," the people said to one another, "the man whom they seek to kill? And here he is, speaking openly, and they say nothing to him."

Jesus was speaking out more boldly than ever: "But I have not come of my own accord; he who sent me is true, and him [he could only mean God] you do not know." At one stage "they sought to arrest him," but did not in fact lay a finger on him. There was something about him that restrained them. And many of the populace said to themselves, "When the Christ appears, will he do more signs than this man has done?"

The antagonism mounted, and the inconclusive struggle continued. The chief priests and Pharisees now sent officers with specific instructions to arrest him. But Jesus was unperturbed. On the last day of the feast, "the great day," he stood up amid them all and proclaimed, "If any one thirsts, let him come to me and drink. He who believes in me, as the scripture has said, 'Out of his heart shall flow rivers of living water.'" The conflict of opinions raged ever more furiously. One point in the argument strikes us curiously. When some people claimed that Jesus was indeed the Christ, others retorted that Christ would not emerge like this from Galilee. "Has not the scripture said that the Christ is descended from David, and comes from Bethlehem?" Such was in fact the case, but for some reason this answer was not provided.

Meanwhile, the chief priests and Pharisees were thoroughly dissatisfied with the officers who had failed to bring off the arrest. These officers had apparently come under the irresistible spell, a point that the Pharisees commented on sarcastically. They complacently added that intellectual and pious persons like themselves had not fallen for this new demagogue. The mob, of course, had proved easy victims.

At this point, Nicodemus, diffident but gallant as always, ventured to speak up for fair play. "Does our law judge a man without first giving him a hearing and learning what he does?" he argued. His colleagues rounded on him bitingly. "Are you from Galilee too? Search and you will see that no prophet is to rise from Galilee." After that everyone went "to their own homes." But Jesus went to the Mount of Olives, where he spent the night.

Next day saw him back in the temple; the people listened to him eagerly. The scribes and Pharisees came forward with what they supposed to be a tricky problem. Today, while we admire both the astuteness and the tenderness of his answer, we regard its purport as so central to Christianity that we cannot imagine Jesus giving any other reply. They brought him a woman "caught in adultery." With extraordinary callousness they placed her in the middle of the company and addressed Jesus with sarcastic deference. "Teacher," they said, "this woman has been caught in the act of adultery. Now in the law Moses commanded us to stone such [meaning stone to death]. What do you say about her?"

Now, there was more guile in this approach than might strike us. Moses did indeed prescribe stoning for adultery, and to say the flat opposite would have involved a direct confrontation with orthodox teaching, which Jesus was not anxious to embark on at that moment. After all, he had come, in his own words, not to abolish the law but to fulfill it. Yet no one with any perception of his character could have supposed that he would support such a penalty for the wretched woman in front of them. There was another point that some of his critics might have considered presented a "teaser." The Romans, the occupying power, had reserved for themselves the imposition of the death penalty, so it was impossible to carry out the Mosaic Law in regard to stoning without breaking the Roman laws.

His interlocutors thought they had worked out all the moves in the game. But he pulled off a fool's mate. To the amazement and bewilderment of all, he bent down and began writing on the ground with his finger. From that day to this, no one has had the faintest idea what he wrote.

It has been suggested that he was indicating that, as God had originally written the law on the two tablets he gave to Moses, he, being divine, could rewrite it. It may or may not be so. A simpler if less ingenious explanation is that he was simply doodling, like a chairman at a meeting showing his disdain for the arguments propounded, while not missing a word. However, they continued to press him. Eventually, he rose up and said with a kind of authoritative indifference:

"Let him who is without sin among you be the first to throw a stone at her." And then, without glancing at them, he bent down again and resumed his doodling.

The woman's persecutors stood dazed, incapable of speech or action. Then "beginning with the eldest," to whom, presumably, the juniors were looking for guidance, they took themselves off. "Slunk off," if the phrase is permitted.

Jesus was left alone with the woman standing before him. He looked up from his strange crouching position and asked her: "Woman, where are they? Has no one condemned you?" "No one, Lord," she replied. "Neither," he said, "do I condemn you; go, and do not sin again."

In any full treatment of Christian forgiveness, this anecdote, a real event after all and not a parable, must hold a place of honor. Jesus generally forgave sins readily, using the expression quite often when he was healing the sick. He was indulgent toward the frailties of his immediate followers. But until he reached the cross, and forgave not only the penitent thief but also his own tormentors and executioners, we find no example so striking as this of the forgiveness of flagrant sinfulness. Much, we recall, was forgiven to the "sinner" who anointed him, because she loved much. But she had not been caught in the middle of an act of adultery, and he was not compelled in that case to provide a debating answer.

The story of the woman taken in adultery is used, sometimes overexploited, to check the condemnation of some public act of immorality, especially sexual immorality. The present writer once availed himself of this very question—which of us is qualified to throw the first stone—on a television epitaph. He was seeking to tone down the execration leveled at a gifted but loose-living man who had just committed suicide. Others have acted, wisely or foolishly, with the same motive. The story will at least remind us always that when we seek to condemn others we should never forget our own sinfulness. But not a few who quote it nowadays are apt to ignore the last part of the last sentence: "Go, and do not sin again." The distinction between loving the sinner and hating the sin could hardly be underlined more clearly.

* * *

There was now no possibility of a compromise, or even a meeting point, with his Jewish opponents as long as they rejected his claims. Some of their questions would have been reasonable enough if directed at anyone else. You bear witness to yourself, they said. Your witness is not true. Why on earth should we suppose that it is? He spelled out his answer in a number of different ways. His judgment, he insisted, was true, for "it is not I alone that judge, but I and he who sent me . . . I bear witness to myself, and the Father who sent me bears witness to me." A little later he put it still more vividly: "When you have lifted up the Son of Man, then you will know that I am he, and that I do nothing on my own authority but speak thus as the Father taught me." We are told that at this point he carried much conviction. "Many believed in him."

Was Jesus near convincing his opponents? One can hardly think so, in spite of his popular support at various moments. We read a little farther on that "the Jews"—meaning no doubt the leaders—asked him insultingly: "Are we not right in saying that you are a Samaritan and have a demon?" A bout of verbal fisticuffs followed, which Jesus ended by saying mysteriously: "Before Abraham was, I am." At that point they took up stones to throw at him. But Jesus "hid himself" and left the temple.

There was no question, however, of their frightening him away, shutting his mouth, or interrupting his work of healing. "As he passed by, he saw a man blind from his birth." The disciples asked him whether the man himself, or his parents, had sinned, thus causing this affliction as punishment. Jesus replied that it was neither, but "the works of God" had to be made manifest in him. Then he went on: "We must work the works of him who sent me, while it is day; night comes when no one can work. As long as I am in the world, I am the light

of the world." Then he proceeded deliberately to perform a
miracle. He spat on the ground, made clay of the spittle, and
anointed the man's eyes with the clay, saying to him: "Go,
wash in the pool of Siloam." The man went off, washed, and
came back able, for the first time in his life, to see.

As a result, a vehement controversy flared up. The formerly
blind man robustly stood up for his benefactor. "Never," he
said, "since the world began has it been heard that any one
opened the eyes of a man born blind." If this man were not
from God, he would have been able to do nothing. But Jesus'
opponents answered him: "You were born in utter sin, and
would you teach us?" They cast him out of the synagogue.
Hearing this, Jesus sought him out and asked him: "Do you
believe in the Son of Man?" The man answered, "And who is
he, sir, that I may believe in him?" Jesus said, "You have seen
him, and it is he who speaks to you." The man said: "Lord, I
believe," and worshiped him from that moment. The sharp
exchanges with the Pharisees continued.

The door of the synagogue had been closed to the man born
blind. Jesus proceeded to explain to the crowd that another
door—spiritual, not material—was opened. "Truly, truly, I say
to you," he cried, "he who does not enter the sheepfold by the
door, but climbs in by another way, that man is a thief and a
robber." In the marvelous imagery that followed, he moved his
own role backward and forward, being at one moment the
door and at the next moment the shepherd. With great emphasis he laid it down: "I am the door of the sheep," and not
just one among the number of doors. In other words, the one
true means of entry and access. "If any one enters by me, he
will be saved, and will go in and out and find pasture." But
almost in alternate sentences he makes the other comparison
between himself and the shepherd: "He who enters by the
door is the shepherd of the sheep. To him the gatekeeper
opens; the sheep hear his voice, and he calls his own sheep by
name and leads them out. When he has brought out all his
own, he goes before them, and the sheep follow him, for they

know his voice." The hireling sees the wolf coming and leaves the sheep and flees, but "I am the good shepherd. The good shepherd lays down his life for the sheep."

Even today, in some parts of Palestine, it is possible to see all this in real life. The village cattle or sheep are fastened up for the night in an enclosure. In the morning each shepherd comes for his own flock and gives his own particular cry, which they recognize. The risks indicated in this story still exist in some places from jackals, wolves, and hyenas. All this would have come home vividly to his audience, who would in any case have been familiar with the frequent comparisons in the Old Testament between God leading his people from slavery to freedom and a devoted shepherd. Psalm 23, beginning: "The Lord is my shepherd, I shall not want," would have been the best known of all.

But what came next must have been disconcerting to his listeners. "And I have other sheep," continued Jesus, "that are not of this fold; I must bring them also, and they will heed my voice. So there shall be one flock, one shepherd." He left them in no doubt that he was proposing to lay down his life and later recover it, not for the Jews only, but for the sake of all mankind. "I lay it down," he concluded, "of my own accord. I have power to lay it down, and I have power to take it again."

The division of opinion became more heated than ever, one group saying that he was possessed of a demon, in fact a lunatic. The other section retorted: "These are not the sayings of one who has a demon. Can a demon open the eyes of the blind?"

8
The Immortal Stories

In the next five months of the Judean ministry, Jesus was to speak the parables which, more than any others, go straight to our hearts. They are unforgettable and permanently affect us. There were fewer miracles performed, or at least recorded in this period, but Jesus' divinity, for those who had eyes to see or who could study the records later, became still more obvious.

Perhaps the most enthralling of all the parables are those of the good Samaritan, the prodigal son, Dives and Lazarus, and the Pharisee and the publican. The first story was probably told before the Feast of Dedication, when Jesus visited Jerusalem, and the other three afterward. But it is the message that is immortal; the dates do not signify greatly.

Despite the violent opposition in Jerusalem, many things were still going well for Jesus. As he went on his way through Judea, he sent ahead seventy "others"—that is to say, disciples other than the apostles. They returned joyfully, exclaiming: "Lord, even the demons are subject to us in your name." We are allowed a rare glimpse of him in a moment of optimism. "In that same hour he rejoiced in the Holy Spirit and said: 'I thank thee, Father, Lord of heaven and earth, that thou hast hidden these things from the wise and understanding and revealed them to babes.'" Turning to the disciples, he said: "Blessed are the eyes that see what you see!" Many prophets and kings had desired such a sight in vain.

But he was not allowed to rest on his laurels for long. A lawyer stood up "to put him to the test." He wanted to know how he might inherit eternal life. Jesus, severely orthodox, asked him what was written on this point in the law. The lawyer answered confidently enough: "You shall love the Lord your God with all your heart, and with all your soul, and with all your strength, and with all your mind; and your neighbor as yourself." Jesus said to him approvingly: "You have answered right, do this, and you will live."

On another occasion, Jesus discussed the same question with a young man who said he had kept the fundamental rules. Jesus told him that if he would be perfect he must give all his goods to the poor and follow the Lord in complete poverty. The young man in question was an earnest seeker after truth, and Jesus, we are told, loved him on sight. He paid him the compliment of demanding of him the almost impossible.

But Jesus evidently saw the lawyer as less idealistic, for the lawyer had continued to debate the matter, as he desired "to justify himself." He persisted, rather like a second-class philosophy tutor, demanding with pseudoinnocence a definition of a word in common use. "And who," he asked, "is my neighbor?" Jesus replied by telling him the story of the good Samaritan, at least as famous as any tale in the New Testament—and perhaps the most famous.

A man was going down from Jerusalem to Jericho—a journey of perhaps thirty-three miles through barren hills and tumbled boulders. He fell among robbers, who stripped him and beat him, leaving him half dead. First a priest and then a Levite happened to go that way, but in each case, as soon as they saw the wretched victim, they passed by on the other side. But

then came a Samaritan. When he saw the man, he had compassion. He went to him and bound up his wounds, pouring in
oil and wine. Then he set him on his own beast and brought
him to an inn and took care of him. But he had not finished his
work of mercy yet, unlike so many of us who accomplish the
occasional good deed and then rush off to celebrate our virtue.
The next day, he took out two denarii (that is, two days'
wages) and gave them to the innkeeper, saying—and this
showed the depth of his generosity—"Take care of him; and
whatever more you spend, I will repay you when I come back."

Now came the leading question to the lawyer: "Which of
these three, do you think, proved neighbor to the man who
fell among the robbers?" He had no option but to answer:
"The one who showed mercy on him." Jesus said to him, not
unkindly, but pointedly: "Go and do likewise."

So, according to Jesus, charity was now to be universal. It
would be unfair and unhistorical to imply that there had been
no glimpse of such a doctrine in the Old Testament, but the
prevailing interpretation of the word "neighbor" was very different. According to one famous Jewish dictum, "an infidel
cannot be a neighbor." That a Samaritan should be selected as
the hero of the parable was astonishing, but no accident, for
the Samaritans were regarded by the Jews with special dislike
and contempt. If Samaritans were to become the models of
charitable conduct, much accepted teaching had to be un-
learned and many deep-rooted prejudices abandoned. A new
conception of the brotherhood of all humanity, irrespective of
race or nation, had to be accepted by the learned and the un-
lettered alike.

* * *

This final period in Judea was not all campaigning. On occa-
sions Jesus found rest and peace in a friendly household in
Bethany, a flourishing little village on the caravan route to
Jericho, an hour's walk from Jerusalem over the Mount of
Olives. We are told simply that as Jesus and his disciples "went

on their way, . . . a woman named Martha received him into her house."

Martha had a sister called Mary, who sat at Jesus' feet and listened to his teaching. But the result was that Martha was "distracted with much serving." Her impatience with the situation was understandable. She did what most other women— or men—would have done in her place. She asked Jesus whether he was quite unconcerned by the fact that all the work was being left to her. "Tell her then to help me," she urged him. Jesus answered her affectionately but firmly. "Martha, Martha, you are anxious and troubled about many things; one thing is needful. Mary has chosen the good portion [or, in some translations, 'the better part'], which shall not be taken away from her."

Here, as so often, Jesus could have made his meaning much plainer, but did not wish to. He has left us to elucidate his thought; and for two thousand years, in this case as in others, the argument has continued. It is easy and not unprofitable to find in his words a spiritual preference for the contemplative, as compared with the active life. But Jesus cannot seriously have been saying that all the housework should have been left undone by both of them, or done solely by Martha. His main point must surely have been that this was a rare spiritual opportunity in enjoyment of which, for the moment, everything should be put aside.

We shall meet Martha and Mary again, and their brother Lazarus. According to some experts, Jesus was able to use the house at Bethany as a home or base from now on. It was certainly most convenient for visits to Jerusalem and for his travels generally.

* * *

By now the Jews had compiled a formidable catalogue of objections to Jesus. He was a Sabbath breaker, to start with, and seemed to set himself above the law. His personal claims, insofar as they were intelligible and not attributable to stark lunacy, had a blasphemous ring. And worst of all, perhaps, he was now saying unmistakably that the Messiah would come to rescue the whole human race and not only the chosen people.

Yet many of them, it seems, were still toying with the possibility that his pretensions might after all be valid. Some gathered around him and asked, "How long will you keep us in suspense? If you are the Christ, tell us plainly." Jesus metaphorically rung his hands. "I told you"—and indeed he had—and still they did not believe. He went on to use words that really could not be misunderstood. "My sheep hear my voice, . . . and I give them eternal life. . . . My Father, who has given them to me, is greater than all, and no one is able to snatch them out of the Father's hand. I and the Father are one."

If "the Jews" (one is never quite sure what proportion of his audience is referred to) were angry before, now they were enraged. Again they took up stones with which to stone him, but still the verbal argument kept them at bay, until he produced yet one more tremendous affirmation. "The Father is in me and I am in the Father." At this point they made a serious effort to arrest him, and yet once again hesitated to take physical action. He withdrew for a while across the Jordan into Perea and stayed there, probably to allow the heat to die down. By March he would be back in Bethany.

* * *

The parable of the prodigal son is a magnificent evocation of the Christian spirit of forgiveness. It is preceded by a shorter parable, also of forgiveness.

We heard earlier from Jesus of the man who left behind ninety-nine of his hundred sheep to find the one that was lost and rejoiced exceedingly when he found it. On that occasion he ended with the moral: "So it is not the will of my Father who is in heaven that one of these little ones should perish." Jesus now expanded this story and concluded with the words: "Just so, I tell you, there will be more joy in heaven over one sinner who repents than over ninety-nine righteous persons who need no repentance." (Compare this with his compelling statement on at least one other occasion: "It is not those who are well who need a physician, but those who are sick. I have not come to call the righteous but sinners to repentance.")

Now begins the main parable. "There was a man," said Jesus, "who had two sons." The younger obtained his "share of the property"—though while the father was alive he had no legal claim—and went off to a "far country" and squandered it there. When he had spent everything and a famine had broken out, he found himself in dire want. He obtained a job feeding swine —to the Jewish hearers this would have been the ultimate degradation—and fed on the husks provided for them. But "no one gave him anything." Eventually he came to his senses; he realized that his situation was much worse than that of his father's hired servants. "I will arise," he said to himself, "and go to my father, and I will say to him, 'Father, I have sinned against heaven and before you: I am no longer worthy to be called your son; treat me as one of your hired servants.'" His remorse was motivated initially by physical suffering and ap-prehension, but was nonetheless genuine for that.

He made his way home but "while he was yet at a distance, his father saw him, and had compassion, and ran and em-braced and kissed him." The prodigal said the words he had prepared, but the father swept all that aside. "Bring quickly," he said to the servants, "the best robe, and put it on him; and put a ring on his hand, and shoes on his feet; and bring the fatted calf and kill it, and let us eat and make merry; for this my son was dead, and is alive again; he was lost, and is found."

We all know how the elder son reacted. "Lo, these many years I have served you," he said, "and I never disobeyed your command; yet you never gave me a kid, that I might make merry with my friends. But when this son of yours came, who has devoured your living with harlots, you killed for him the fatted calf." The father's answer epitomized Christian tender-ness to the respectable and the not so respectable alike. "Son," he said, "you are always with me, and all that is mine is yours. It was fitting to make merry and be glad, for this your brother was dead, and is alive; he was lost and is found."

Is there anything to be said about this immortal story that has not been said a thousand times? One thing perhaps about the activity of the father in question, who is after all the key figure in this record of Christian forgiveness. The father ran and embraced the prodigal son, feeling compassion for him while he was still at a distance, even before he could be by any means certain that the son had really repented. It is too easy for Christians to think of forgiveness as a negative quality, either a mere absence of resentment or at best a readiness to wipe the slate clean when the initiative has been taken by the penitent. In the story of the prodigal son we are given a picture of true Christian forgiveness that is above all positive and that carries us forward to embrace the prodigal son without waiting for him to fall at our feet.

Another of the great parables is that of Dives and Lazarus. "There was a rich man, who was clothed in purple and fine linen and who feasted sumptuously every day. And at his gate lay a poor man named Lazarus, full of sores, who desired to be fed with what fell from the rich man's table; moreover, the dogs came and licked his sores."

The poor man died and was carried by the angels to Abraham's bosom. The rich man also died and found himself in Hades. Being in torment he lifted up his eyes, saw Abraham, and Lazarus in his bosom, and called out: "Father Abraham, have mercy upon me, and send Lazarus to dip the end of his finger in water and cool my tongue; for I am in anguish in this flame." But Abraham made a chilly response. He reminded Dives that he had had a good time in his lifetime and Lazarus a bad one. Now the situations were reversed. A great chasm had been fixed between them that no one could cross. Dives begged that at least Lazarus might be sent to warn his five brothers. Abraham pointed out that they had Moses and the prophets, and if they did not heed them they would not be convinced even by someone who had risen from the dead.

By the end of the story most of us probably feel sympathy for Dives, particularly in his desire to help his brothers, and something less than goodwill toward Father Abraham. According to our modern ways of thought, Dives, even if uninterested in social welfare during his lifetime, had at least repented. The main lesson driven home is the utter irrelevance of good or bad fortune in this world to our eternal destiny, which depends upon our behavior during our earthly life.

Finally, the parable of the Pharisee and the publican. Two men went up into the temple to pray, one a Pharisee and the other a publican (a tax collector). The Pharisee prayed contentedly enough. "God, I thank thee that I am not like other men, extortioners, unjust, adulterers, or even [with a patronizing glance] like this tax collector. I fast twice a week, I give tithes of all that I get." But the publican, "standing far off, would not even lift up his eyes to heaven, but beat his breast, saying: 'God, be merciful to me a sinner.'" "This man," said Jesus, "went down to his house justified rather than the other." Then comes the generalized moral: "For every one who exalts himself will be humbled, but he who humbles himself will be exalted." A large part of the Christian doctrine of humility is contained in that one sentence.

* * *

The shadow of the inescapable climax was beginning to fall. But Jesus had still to perform the most resounding of all his miracles. He had already raised two young people from the dead—the daughter of Jairus and the son of the widow of Naim. Something still more dramatic and public was coming.

In March A.D. 30 Jesus was somewhere east of the Jordan— so to speak, out of the danger zone—when an anxious message reached him from the two sisters of Bethany, Martha and Mary, about their brother Lazarus. "Lord," they sent word to him, "he whom you love [Lazarus] is ill." Jesus, we are told specifically, loved Martha and Mary, so all three must have been dear to him, but his first comment was undisturbed enough and to his hearers somewhat mysterious. "This illness," he said, "is not unto death; it is for the glory of God, so that the Son of God may be glorified by means of it." He seemed to indicate that there was no immediate need for action, and for two days longer he stayed where he was.

Then, without apparent reason, his attitude seemed to change. "Let us go into Judea again," he said to his disciples. Understandably, they demurred. They pointed out that it was not long since the Jews had been trying to stone him to death. Surely it was madness to put his head back into their noose. He used words that suggested he had little time left to perform works of mercy, and continued, "Our friend Lazarus has fallen asleep, but I go to awake him out of sleep." It was as though he had received some fresh news through an invisible channel. The disciples, as usual, took his words literally. "Lord," they said, "if he has fallen asleep, he will recover." Jesus then broke the news to them plainly. "Lazarus is dead; . . . let us go to him." Thomas, who had been described as a habitual pessimist, was here, as in his later life, uncompromisingly brave. "Let us also go," he said, "that we may die with him."

By the time Jesus and his party reached Bethany, Lazarus had already been in the tomb four days. Martha, the busy, enterprising one, hastened to meet Jesus, while Mary, tranquil as always, remained at home. Martha greeted Jesus with the words: "Lord, if you had been here, my brother would not have died." Even now it was not too late. She knew that God would grant Jesus anything he asked. Jesus assured Martha that her brother would rise again. But that was not sufficient for her, though she acknowledged, "I know that he will rise again in the resurrection at the last day." Then Jesus said to her: "I am the resurrection and the life; he who believes in me, though he die, yet shall he live, and whoever lives and believes in me shall never die." He asked her whether she believed this. Her reply was unqualified. "Yes, Lord; I believe that you are the Christ, the Son of God, he who is coming into the world."

Martha rushed off to fetch Mary. Mary fell at Jesus' feet using the same words as Martha: "Lord, if you had been here, my brother would not have died." When Jesus saw her weeping, and the Jews who came with her also weeping, "he was deeply moved in spirit and troubled." He asked the simple question: "Where have you laid him?" They said to him: "Lord, come and see." Curiously enough, these are the first words ever attributed to Jesus in St. John's gospel. Now comes the shortest verse in the gospels. "Jesus wept." The bystanders were impressed with his profound affection: "See how he loved him." But the question was mooted whether this supreme miracle worker ought not to have been able to prevent the tragedy.

Jesus, "deeply moved again," came to the tomb. It was a cave, and a stone blocked the entrance. Jesus said: "Take away the stone." Martha warned him that the smell of the dead man would by now be very unpleasant. Jesus assured her that those who believed would see the glory of God. So the stone was removed. The miracle that followed received a more solemn prelude than any other. He lifted up his eyes and said: "Father, I thank thee that thou hast heard me." He felt it necessary to say this publicly, so that the people might indeed believe that God had sent him. Then he cried with a loud voice: "Lazarus! Come out!" The dead man came out, his hands and feet bound with bandages and his face wrapped with a cloth. Jesus finished with the matter-of-fact instruction: "Unbind him, and let him go."

This provoked another division of opinion among the Jews. Many of the spectators "believed in him," but some went off to the Pharisees with a report and a warning. The chief priests and the Pharisees "gathered the council" and decided to tackle in earnest the problem that Jesus presented. It was pointed out that if he went on like this everyone would come to believe in him; the Romans would be thoroughly alarmed: They "will come and destroy both our holy places and our nation." Caiaphas, however, who was the high priest that year, treated their agitation with disdain. "You know nothing at all," he said to them. "You do not understand that it is expedient for you that one man should die for the people, and that the whole nation should not perish."

The Jews understood. From that day on, they plotted actively to bring about his death. Jesus once again decided that the moment was not ripe for the ultimate confrontation. He withdrew "to the country near the wilderness, to a town called Ephraim." He stayed there for a while with his disciples.

* * *

But the pause was not prolonged. The time had now come for which his whole life had been a preparation. "Behold," he said, "we are going up to Jerusalem; and the Son of Man will be delivered to the chief priests and scribes, and they will condemn him to death, and deliver him to the Gentiles; and they will mock him, and spit upon him, and scourge him, and kill him; and after three days he will rise." They set off together on the journey to martyrdom. But his companions remained all too humanly frail. Jesus had one final chance to preach humility.

James and John, the sons of Zebedee, came to him with a naïve request. "Grant us," they begged him, "to sit, one at your right hand and one at your left, in your glory." Jesus told them that they simply did not understand what they were asking. Were they able to drink his cup, or be baptized with his baptism? They replied unhesitatingly: "We are able." Jesus answered them in a way that was a kind of compliment, but at the same time destroyed any crude idea of their preferment in a future kingdom. "The cup that I drink you will drink; and with the baptism with which I am baptized, you will be baptized; but to sit at my right hand or at my left is not mine to grant, but it is for those for whom it has been prepared."

The other apostles were indignant with James and John, but Jesus set the whole thing quietly in perspective. In the Gentile world great men exercised authority over lesser men, but it should not be so among his disciples. "Whoever would be great among you must be your servant, and whoever would be first among you must be slave of all. For the Son of Man also came not to be served but to serve, and to give his life as a ransom for many." By this time he may be said to have summed up here the full Christian doctrine of humility, starting with the idea of humility as the recognition of one's own lowliness in front of God and culminating in the idea of humility as service.

Jesus continued his journey through Jericho, healing Bartimeus, the blind beggar, and welcoming the hospitality of Zaccheus, the tax gatherer, "small of stature," who climbed into a sycamore tree to see him.

Six days before the Passover—that is, on the Saturday before Good Friday—he came back to the familiar house in Bethany. As usual, Martha served and Lazarus was "one of those at table with them." Mary, not for the first time, behaved in a manner all her own. She took a pound of costly ointment and anointed the feet of Jesus and wiped his feet with her hair. And the house was filled with the fragrance of the ointment. Her action as described was so like that of the sinner referred to earlier that some have concluded that there was one episode, not two. But on balance, they seem to be wrong.

Judas Iscariot then stepped forward with an unpleasant question. "Why was this ointment not sold for three hundred denarii and given to the poor?" Jesus came to her defense at once. "Why do you trouble her?" he said. "She has done a beautiful thing to me. For you always have the poor with you, . . . but you will not always have me." In pouring the ointment on his body, she had prepared him for burial. And in a prediction fulfilled beyond question he concluded: "Wherever the gospel is preached in the whole world, what she has done will be told in memory of her."

And so they reached Palm Sunday.

9
"O Jerusalem!"

The Passover was the greatest Jewish festival, commemorating God's deliverance of the Israelites from the "tenth plague," which killed all the first-born sons of the Egyptians. For seven days Jews were to eat unleavened bread and consecrate all their time to God.

The second of April would have come at a lovely time in Judea. We can think of it as in all senses a glorious day. Jesus and his disciples passed along the lower slopes of the Mount of Olives, leaving the summit on their left. When they approached the small village of Bethphage he told his disciples to go into the village. They would find an "ass tied, and a colt with her." They should "untie them and bring them to me." "If any one says anything to you, you shall say, 'The Lord has need of them.'" The owner would at once respond. All went smoothly. The disciples placed some of their clothing on the ass and the colt and Jesus "sat thereon." This, we are told by St. Matthew (and also by St. John), was to fulfill the prophecy of Zachariah:

> Tell the daughter of Zion,
> Behold, your king is coming to you,
> humble, and mounted on an ass,
> and on a colt, the foal of an ass.

The selection of this particular prophecy by the two evangelists is of great significance. The Jesus of this day of triumph was, as they looked back, the gentle Jesus riding on the ass, a recognized symbol of peace and simplicity.

But it does not seem that the multitude who soon collected saw it that way at all. They came together to welcome and accompany him in large numbers as he drew near to Jerusalem. Many of them would have been local inhabitants already excited by the raising of Lazarus, and many others pilgrims come together for the Passover, including a strong contingent from Galilee. Some cut branches from the trees and spread them on the road, and others laid down their garments. The crowds all around him cried out triumphantly. "Hosanna to the Son of David! Blessed is he who comes in the name of the Lord! Hosanna in the highest!" Obviously they did not understand the meaning of the lowly ass. To all who asked what was going on, they replied: "This is the prophet Jesus from Nazareth of Galilee."

Professor Dodd cogently reminds us of the famous passage in the psalms:

Behold O Lord! and raise up their King, the Son of David . . .
In wisdom, in justice may you thrust out sinners from God's
    heritage,
blot out the lawless Gentiles with a word,
put the Gentiles to flight with his threats.

He suggests that we should substitute "Romans," the hated occupiers of their country, for "Gentiles" in the quotation, in order to assess the demonstration at its true value. The mood was one of militant nationalism. Here, at last, was the Messiah, the liberator, whom they had so long awaited. Feeling ran high among the swollen populace.

Soon the glittering city of Jerusalem lay before Jesus, and while the multitude exulted almost hysterically, he found the sight unbearably poignant, and wept over it, saying: "Would that even today you knew the things that make for peace! But now they are hid from your eyes." The days would come when their enemies would surround them and destroy them and their children. "They will not leave one stone upon another in you: because you did not know the time of your visitation." But it does not seem that the ardor of the crowd was diminished.

He made straight for the temple and in a moment was driving out all who bought and sold there. He had performed the same operation two years earlier, but this time he had many more allies and temporary acolytes. He overturned the tables of the money changers and the seats of those who sold pigeons. "Is it not written," he said, according to St. Mark, " 'My house shall be called a house of prayer for all the nations'? But you have made it a den of robbers."

This phrase "den of robbers" may give a false impression. The charge was not one of dishonest trading, nor merely one of introducing commerce into holy places—though this was involved—but one of exploiting a high and unique privilege for selfish ends. The Son of David was expected to cleanse Jerusalem from the Gentiles. Jesus wanted to cleanse it *for* the Gentiles, but this can hardly have been understood at the time. The exercise was no doubt taken at its face value as an assault on blatant pollution.

That night he returned to the house of Martha, Mary, and Lazarus in Bethany. During the day he had healed many sick persons and been widely acclaimed. On the surface at least all had gone well.

Jesus himself was not carried away by the euphoria surrounding him for a moment. Next day he set to work to bring out the somber truth. "Now among those who went up to worship at the feast were some Greeks." They approached the apostle Philip, who came from Bethsaida, at the north end of the Sea of Galilee, which was fairly close to the Greek cities in Decapolis, from which these Greek pilgrims may have come. They may have been a little uncertain of their reception by Jesus, but Philip, assisted by Andrew, had no difficulty in arranging for Jesus to see them. For whatever reason, he chose to speak to them with exceptional plainness. "The hour has come for the Son of Man to be glorified," he said. And then he drove in the ineluctable message that self-fulfillment is impossible without self-repudiation. He had already taught his disciples that "He who loves his life loses it, and he who hates his life in this world will keep it for eternal life." He said that again to the Greeks, but now he illustrated his meaning with incomparable phrasing: "Truly, truly, I say to you, unless a grain of wheat falls into the earth and dies, it remains alone; but if it dies, it bears much fruit."

We can see this as the principle of life through death. It is a principle that lies at the heart of the gospel; and it was characteristic of Jesus that he should have drawn his image from nature, which is itself a demonstration of divine power. In the parable of the sower, Jesus had talked of the wheat that falls on good ground and bears fruit, thirty, sixty, or a hundredfold. But now he explained that however good the soil, the seed does not achieve its true destiny without dying on the way. The Greeks had recognized that sacrifice might be necessary in the interest of the community. What they had never understood was that the mutual sacrifice that expresses mutual love is itself most joyous. This, according to Archbishop Temple, is the vital point at which the ethics of the gospel leave the ethics of Greek philosophy far behind.

Jesus did not conceal the fact that his soul was "troubled." "What shall I say," he asked himself anxiously. " 'Father, save me from this hour'?" No, he would not do that, for this hour was the culmination of his whole mission and the essential reason why he had entered the world. No, he would say,

"Father, glorify thy name." And a voice came from heaven, "I have glorified it, and I will glorify it again."

The crowd was awestruck but unclear what had happened. Had it thundered or had he been addressed by an angel? Jesus told them: "This voice has come for your sake, not for mine. Now is the judgment of this world, now shall the ruler of this world be cast out; and I, when I am lifted up from the earth, will draw all men to myself." He was, as we are all now aware, referring to his crucifixion. But the crowd was, if anything, still more bewildered. Jesus left them a final message, which each man could interpret for himself. "The light," he said, "is with you for a little longer. . . . While you have the light, believe in the light, that you may become sons of light." We are told that by this time many "even of the authorities believed in him, but for fear of the Pharisees they did not confess it." Jesus was very much aware of the hostility in high places, and almost for the last time he thought it prudent to hide himself, and withdrew once again to Bethany.

The last few days before Jesus' arrest were to be filled by strenuous debate with his opponents, and utterances made more poignant by the closeness of the moment of sacrifice. By Tuesday the battle was well and truly joined. The evangelists do not clearly attribute particular events to particular days, but it is probable that the Tuesday of Holy Week was the occasion for the last great public utterances. These did not all take the form of denunciations. There was the affecting moment when Jesus looked up "and saw the rich putting their gifts into the treasury; and he saw a poor widow put in two copper coins [which we are accustomed to refer to as a mite]. And he said, 'Truly I tell you, this poor widow has put in more than all of them; for they all contributed out of their abundance, but she out of her poverty put in all the living that she had.' "

But most of the recorded sayings were of a combative character. After all, the Jews could hardly have been expected not to retaliate after the cleansing of the temple.

Not surprisingly, the Jews raised with him again the crucial questions of authority, theirs and his. Their whole *raison d'être* depended on the double assumption that true authority resided in the law of Moses and that it could rightly be exercised by themselves as his legitimate successors. "Tell us by what authority you do these things," they said. "Who is it who gave you this authority?" Jesus answered this debating question with another. What did they make of John the Baptist? Was he or was he not a genuine prophet sent from God? The Pharisees had not cared for John, but he was far too popular to be crudely repudiated. "We do not know," they feebly answered. Then, said Jesus, "Neither will I tell you by what authority I do these things." But when he quoted the prophetic saying that the house of God should be "a house of prayer for all the nations," he had left the official world in no doubt that he was challenging their religious monopoly.

Jesus' public utterances became more pointed. He told the parable of the householder who planted a vineyard and set a hedge around it; he dug a winepress in it, built a tower, and then went into another country. When he sent his servants to obtain the fruit, they were successively beaten and killed. Finally he sent his son, saying to himself, "They will respect my son." But the tenants did not. "This," they said to themselves, "is the heir; come, let us kill him and have his inheritance." So they killed him in his turn.

Having gotten as far as this with the parable, Jesus was not going to let his listeners off lightly. He asked them, "When the owner of the vineyard comes, what will he do to those tenants?" They answered with remarkable naïveté. He would put those wretches to a miserable death and let out the vineyard to other tenants, who would give him the fruits in their seasons. Jesus' *coup de grâce* was as obvious as it was crushing. "I tell you, the kingdom of God will be taken away from you and given to a nation producing the fruits of it."

In one of the hard-hitting debates of this last week, Jesus brilliantly indicated the true limits of political obligations. He was asked, "Is it lawful to pay taxes to Caesar or not?" He requested a coin, and holding it up, asked them as so often the simplest of questions: "Whose likeness and inscription is this?" "Caesar's," they replied. Then he said to them, "Render therefore to Caesar the things that are Caesar's, and to God the things that are God's." Sometimes his withering replies provoked his opponents to attempt violence, but this time they seemed satisfied with his answer. They marveled, left him, and went away.

Soon Jesus was pitching into the scribes and Pharisees, at least as they had come to present themselves to the people. "Woe to you scribes and Pharisees," he repeated four times with many embellishments, "Woe to you, blind guides," "You serpents, you brood of vipers."

But one is always aware that while his anger was unmitigated, his sorrow went deeper still. "O Jerusalem, Jerusalem," he cried, standing on the steps of the temple, "killing the prophets and stoning those who are sent to you! How often would I have gathered your children together as a hen gathers her brood under her wings, and you would not!"

He had left the temple and was setting off when his disciples asked him whether he was not impressed by the magnificence of the building. Yet once again he disconcerted them with his answer. "Truly, I say to you, there will not be left here one stone upon another that will not be thrown down." And when they reached the Mount of Olives he drew a terrible picture of the last days. "For nation will rise against nation, and kingdom against kingdom, and there will be famines and earthquakes in various places. All this is but the beginning of the birth pangs." The sun would be darkened and the moon would give no light. All the tribes of the earth would see the Son of Man coming on the clouds of heaven with power and great glory. The disciples would have to be prepared for every kind of tribulation. "You will be hated by all for my name's sake." They would be put to death. But he who endured to the end would be saved—if not in this world, then in whatever state of being came afterward.

Jesus continued to concentrate his attention and that of his listeners on the final judgment. In the parable of the wise and foolish virgins, those who took oil for their lamps were able to attend the wedding, while those who failed to do so found themselves left outside. In the parable of the talents, those who made use of whatever talents came their way "entered into the joy of their master," but the one who was only given one talent and hid it in the ground was cast into outer darkness. The moral, one supposes, is that it is not for us to decide whether our endowment here is just or otherwise, but to make use of it to the full, whatever we think of it.

And so to the parable of the sheep and the goats. It contains a passage that has probably inspired more labor and sacrifice on behalf of the stricken and handicapped than any other. On the last day the King would invite those on his right hand—the sheep in the story—to share with him the kingdom. "For I was hungry and you gave me food, I was thirsty and you gave me drink, I was a stranger and you welcomed me, I was naked and you clothed me, I was sick and you visited me, I was in prison and you came to me." They would ask him when they had performed these acts of charity to him, and he would reply: "As you did it to one of the least of these my brethren, you did it to me." If it were not that the Crucifixion and Resurrection had still to come, those would have been wonderful last words.

Jesus probably remained at Bethany on the Wednesday, summoning up his spiritual energies for the supreme ordeal. But the priests, to whom the scribes and Pharisees seem to have passed the responsibilities for dealing with their all too powerful adversary, realized that they would have to act quickly—if possible, before the Passover, which was now very close at hand. The city was already filling up with pilgrims, many of whom might sympathize with Jesus.

At this point Judas Iscariot made his secret deal with the

religious authorities to betray his master. It was very convenient for them to be told where and when Jesus could be found and how he could be arrested with the least possible disturbance. But even without Judas they would no doubt have achieved their purpose.

10
Preparing for Sacrifice

Jesus had said more than once that his hour had not yet come. But now the hour indubitably *had* come. Jesus knew it with certainty. Some inkling must have seeped through to the others.

The final meeting of all the apostles was at the Last Supper. Argument still rages as to whether this was an actual celebration of the feast of the Passover or a supper of equal solemnity occurring on the previous day, which took its place. It does not matter a great deal. In either case, the arrangements made by Jesus were simple but effective, like those that preceded his entry into Jerusalem. "Go," he said to some of his disciples, "into the city, and a man carrying a jar of water will meet you; follow him, and wherever he enters, say to the householder, 'The Teacher [or may one here translate it "Master"?] says, Where is my guest room, where I am to eat the Passover with my disciples?'" He would show them a large upper room furnished and ready. They should prepare the Passover there, which they duly did.

Jesus, who "loved his own" throughout, resolved to demonstrate it in some special fashion now. They had so little time left together. An opportunity was not long in coming.

There was at the Supper another of those humiliating disputes among them as to which was to be regarded as the greatest. Jesus taught them yet again the familiar lesson of humility, presenting it not merely as a negative virtue but as a positive inspiration to service. "Let the greatest among you," he said, "become as the youngest; and the leader as one who serves. For which is the greater, one who sits at table, or one who serves? Is it not the one who sits at table? But I am among you as one who serves."

He now put his words into practice. He rose from supper, laid aside his garments, and girded himself with a towel. "Then he poured water into a basin, and began to wash the disciples' feet, and to wipe them with the towel with which he was girded." Peter protested that it was all wrong for Jesus to wash *his* feet, but Jesus gently explained to him that unless he washed Peter's feet, Peter could "have no part in him."

But at this point we hear (the phrase has been employed before) that Jesus was troubled in spirit. He felt bound to warn the disciples that one of them would betray him. The disciples were dumfounded, as well they might have been. All those at table were reclining on their left elbows. St. John, the beloved disciple, on Jesus' right hand, would have had his head not far from Jesus' breast. Peter made some gesture to John to find out to whom Jesus was referring. John asked Jesus who it was and was told in reply, "It is he to whom I shall give this morsel when I have dipped it." Dipping a choice morsel was held to represent a mark of favor. Jesus dipped the morsel and gave it to Judas.

Jesus was surely making a last appeal to what was good in Judas, but Satan, we are told, entered Judas; whatever that may mean precisely, the Hyde in him visibly triumphed over the Jekyll. Jesus told him to do what he had in mind quickly. He rose and went outside "and it was night." St. John explains to us that the other disciples thought that Judas, their treasurer, was receiving some financial instruction from Jesus. We are left to assume that no one except St. John heard Jesus explaining the meaning of the dipped morsel, that St. John kept it to himself for the time being, and that Peter did not pursue his question about the identity of the traitor. It would be answered soon enough by events.

The supreme happening at the Last Supper was the institution of the Eucharist. St. John does not mention it, an interesting example of what he does *not* think it necessary to describe. Writing long after Matthew, Mark, and Luke, he would not concern himself to record what by that time was taken for granted. The other three evangelists and St. Paul (in his first epistle to the Corinthians) differ in minor ways, but there is no doubt about the substantial similarity and intended significance of all their accounts.

As they were eating, Jesus (according to St. Matthew) "took bread, and blessed, and broke it, and gave it to the disciples and said, 'Take, eat, this is my body.'" St. Luke adds, "which is given for you. Do this in remembrance of me." In the same way after supper he took the cup and gave it to them saying: "Drink of it, all of you, for this is my blood of the covenant [according to St. Luke, 'the new covenant'], which is poured out for many for the forgiveness of sins." No words in human history have been so remorselessly mulled over and debated. In this context we must remember what Jesus said earlier, the day after he had performed the miracle of the feeding of the five thousand. "I am the bread of life. He who eats my flesh and drinks my blood lives forever."

With the supreme rite established and Judas departed, Jesus seemed to speak more freely, almost with exhilaration. He mentioned without inhibition the glorification of God and the Son of Man and continued: "Little children, yet a little while I am with you." As he had said earlier, he was going shortly where they could not follow him. He then delivered as much of his ethical teaching as could be impressed into a single sentence: "A new commandment I give to you, that you love one another; even as I have loved you." They should be ready to be judged by the extent to which they lived up to this standard. "How these Christians loved one another" is a phrase used sarcastically. The sarcasm is justified all too often, but the ideal remains unsullied.

We must think of Simon Peter as a man who found it difficult to keep quiet for very long at a time. Now he burst out with a reasonable question: "Lord, where are you going?" Jesus replied, still a shade enigmatically, still anxious to provoke spiritual searching rather than handout textbook answers. "Where I am going you cannot follow me now; but you shall follow afterward." Peter asserted heatedly that he would follow him to the ends of the earth and lay down his life for him. Jesus replied with painful prescience: "Will you lay down your life for me? . . . the cock will not crow, till you have denied me three times."

Then, or soon afterward, Jesus embarked on an exposition of Christian theology and ethics unequaled even by the Sermon on the Mount for the extent of its total revelation. Filling four tight-packed chapters of St. John (14–17), it would be almost blasphemous to imply that it could be effectively summarized. But we must not neglect some of the high points.

Whatever mystical truths we look for in the message today, the predominant note at the time must have been reassurance. Jesus was leaving them; this he had to tell them baldly. But if only they could understand the true prospect, there would be no reason whatever for sadness. After all, he said a shade surprisingly, they knew where he was going, "to prepare a place for them." Perhaps he meant they *ought* to know by this time. Thomas protested that they had no idea where he was going. How could they possibly know the way? Jesus replied with a resounding affirmation: "I am the way, and the truth, and the life." He added that since they knew him they knew his father also, and the world of heaven should no longer be a closed book to them. Philip persisted in begging to be shown the Father. Jesus made the same point that he had just made to

Thomas. "He who has seen me has seen the Father." And he added the mystical corollary, "Do you not believe that I am in the Father and the Father in me?"

The themes in this discourse become increasingly interwoven. At one moment Jesus' emphasis was immediate and ethical: "If you love me, you will keep my commandments." At another he was concentrating on the spiritual future: "I will pray the Father, and he will give you another Counselor, to be with you forever." A number of phrases and statements relate to the last-named. He is the spirit of truth, the Holy Spirit, "whom the Father will send in my name." He "proceeds from the Father, he will bear witness to me." "It is to your advantage that I go away, for if I do not go away, the Counselor will not come to you; but if I go, I will send him to you."

He made another promise that must have meant even more to them at that moment: "I will come again," he said, "and will take you to myself; that where I am, you may be also." It has been claimed that there are three hundred references to the Second Coming in the New Testament. St. Peter gives the most vivid picture: "The day of the Lord will come like a thief and then the heavens will pass away with a loud noise and the elements will be dissolved with fire, and the earth and the works that are upon it will be burned up." The precise significance of the Second Coming may be disputed, but there is no questioning its biblical credentials.

On another plane of thought, Jesus indicated that the Father and he himself were always available: "If a man loves me, he will keep my word, and my Father will love him, and we will come to him and make our home with him." On this level the idea of movement among the three divine persons of the Trinity is transcended in favor of a permanent presence. "I am the true vine, and my Father is the vinedresser . . . I am the vine, you are the branches." But he always moves back to the world of practical duties, the terrible ordeal in front of him, and the unfailing guarantees of divine sustenance. "Ask, and you will receive, that your joy may be full." "I have said this to you, that in me you may have peace. In the world you have tribulation; but be of good cheer, I have overcome the world."

The last great prayer for his disciples contained the phrases most often used, and quite rightly, in ecumenical orations. "I do not pray for these only, but also for those who believe in me through their word, that they may all be one; even as thou, Father, art in me, and I in thee, that they also may be in us." But the limitless range and depth of Jesus' love for his apostles and for all humanity are perhaps brought out best of all in two other sentences in the same chapter. "I am coming to thee; and these things I speak in the world, that they may have my joy fulfilled in themselves. . . . And for their sake I consecrate myself, that they also may be consecrated in truth."

* * *

The supper and the discourse ended. The little party made their way across the brook, Kedron, to a place called Gethsemane. It lay on the slopes of the Mount of Olives across the valley from the east gate of the city. Jesus said to his disciples, other than Peter, James, and John, "Sit here, while I pray." These three he took on a little farther, but then he halted them also. "My soul is very sorrowful, even to death," he said, "remain here and watch." Or, in another translation, "My heart is ready to break with sorrow." He went forward alone and threw himself on his knees in prayer.

Theologians and others have speculated throughout the ages and will continue to speculate about the precise nature of Jesus' agony. His all too precise foreknowledge of the physical horror in store for him must certainly have afflicted his human nature, but it was probably by no means the most distressing element. We must assume that he felt more poignantly than ever before the full burden of the world's guilt, including the guilt of those who were about to crucify him.

Sweat poured from him like great drops of blood while he prayed that if it were possible the cup should pass from him. "Nevertheless not as I will, but as thou wilt." He returned to the three apostles and found them sleeping. He said to Peter, "So, could you not watch with me one hour? Watch and pray that you may not enter into temptation; the spirit indeed is willing, but the flesh is weak." He resumed his prayer, but this time still more resigned to his destiny. "My Father, if this cannot pass unless I drink it, thy will be done." Again he found the three disciples sleeping. Once more he resumed his prayers, and then he roused the disciples in earnest. It was time to be moving. "See, my betrayer is at hand."

Judas was accompanied by a great crowd with swords and clubs from the chief priests and elders of the people, though it would be the Roman soldiers who effected the arrest. He kissed Jesus, a prearranged signal to indicate the eminent victim. The phrase that he used seems to us particularly nauseating: "Hail, Master!" But who knows what extraordinary feelings of guilt he was suffering. Jesus replied to him mildly enough, "Friend, why are you here?" Could it be that it was at that moment that Judas was overtaken by the remorse that led him to try to repay the blood money and take his own life soon afterward? Peter at least showed an admirable physical courage. He drew his sword and struck off the ear of Malchus, the high priest's servant. Jesus, however, performed his last act of healing. He restored the ear with a touch and once more tried to teach the difference between physical and spiritual values. "Put your sword back in its place," he said to Peter, "for all who take the sword will perish by the sword." If he wished he could call on his heavenly father for twelve legions of angels, but how then "should the scriptures be fulfilled"? Thereupon he allowed himself to be led away, like a lamb to the slaughter. Throughout what follows, we must understand the tactics of the Jewish leaders. The disciples, deprived of the only method of defending him they understood, took to their heels and fled.

❋   ❋   ❋

A preliminary hearing was held before Annas, the former high priest. Then came Jesus' two trials. One was before the Jewish court, one before the Roman governor; each ended in a condemnation on a capital charge, but a different charge in each case.

The Sanhedrin, before whom Jesus first appeared, saw itself as the sovereign assembly of Israel, alone authorized to administer the law handed down from Moses. But as Judea was a Roman province, the Sanhedrin was a municipal organ of administration with legal powers no wider than those that Rome chose to allow it. The Roman governor, Pontius Pilate, kept the death penalty in his own hands.

The Jewish leaders had a double purpose. They were determined not only to secure the execution of Jesus but also to discredit his prophetic claims in the minds of the populace. For the first purpose Pontius Pilate was the indispensable instrument, but for the religious destruction of Jesus' reputation, their own condemnation was essential. What they needed was a judicial outcome that would be equally effective for their political and religious purposes.

The leaders of the Sanhedrin were apparently successful. They obtained an admission from Jesus that enabled them to convict him of blasphemy, a capital offense in Jewish law, though not one that they had the power under the Romans to punish with death. At the same time they extracted an apparent claim on his part to be King of the Jews, in a sense that enabled them to present him as a dangerous rebel against the Romans. They had done quite a good job for their cause—or so it seemed at the time.

11
Crucifixion

The arrest was made by Roman soldiers accompanied by the temple police, which suggests that it was treated as quite a serious operation. They brought Jesus, his hands bound, in the first place to Annas, the father-in-law of Caiaphas, the high priest, and himself a former holder of the office.

St. John alone describes the informal preliminary investigation. Jesus was questioned by Annas about his disciples and his teaching. He replied that he had spoken openly before the world. Why not ask those who had heard him? This sort of answer did not please one of the officers, who struck Jesus with his open hand. Was this, he demanded, the way to answer the (former) high priest? Jesus replied mildly enough, "If I have spoken wrongly, bear witness to the wrong; but if I have spoken rightly, why do you strike me?" So Annas, making no headway, sent Jesus on to Caiaphas. It must have been at this point that the men who were holding Jesus mocked and beat him, blindfolded him, and shouted, "Prophesy! Who is it who struck you?"

Jesus had been arrested in the middle of the night. The

formal trial for which the Sanhedrin had to be mobilized took place in the early hours of the morning. It had to be finished by 6 A.M., when the feast day started. The chief priests and the council immediately showed that they were looking for the kind of evidence required by the Mosaic law to enable them to pass a death sentence. Unfortunately, none was forthcoming. There were plenty of witnesses, it is true, but their evidence was full of mutual contradictions too glaring even for the Sanhedrin. At last some men came forward who seemed more promising. They were ready to swear that Jesus had said that he would destroy the temple made with hands and within three days raise another one not made with hands. This, though a perversion of the truth, deliberate or otherwise, came somewhere near to what Jesus had actually said. But even here there was no agreement among the witnesses about the words used.

Caiaphas assumed a judicial air and asked Jesus severely how he answered the charges against him. But Caiaphas was too intelligent not to be aware that there was no case to answer. When Jesus maintained an impassive silence, Caiaphas realized that with time running out he would have to take on the job himself. He adopted what seems to us now the obvious line of questioning.

Putting together the slightly different accounts given in the gospels, it is clear that Caiaphas asked two related but distinguishable questions. Are you the Christ—in other words, the Messiah? Are you the Son of God? Jesus indicated assent to both questions, and added with calculated audacity, "But I tell you, hereafter you will see the Son of Man seated at the right hand of Power, and coming on the clouds of heaven."

The claim to messiahship would not necessarily have been blasphemous, but presenting himself as the Son of Man invested with divine attributes would inevitably have been so regarded. Whatever his precise reasoning, the high priest had now obtained the material he needed for a religious condemnation. But political charges were necessary for the death

sentence. These were duly trumped up: Jesus had disturbed
the people, condemned the payment of tribute, and proclaimed himself King. He was led away, bound, to Pilate.

Meanwhile, against the background of the world-embracing
ordeals of Jesus, there had developed the personal tragedy of
Simon Peter. It will be recalled that he had promised to remain faithful to death; that he had lashed out on Jesus' behalf
at the time of the arrest to find himself rebuked, however
gently, for excessive zeal; that he had then fled with the others.
His whole being was permeated with love of his master. He
could not desert him for long. He now made his way to the
edge of the trial, accompanied by another apostle, no doubt
St. John.

According to St. Matthew, Peter was sitting "outside in the
courtyard" when a maid came up to him and said, "You also
were with Jesus the Galilean." Peter denied it before them all,
asserting, "I do not know what you mean." He went out to the
porch; another maid made the same allegation, and again he
repudiated it, this time with an oath. But the bystanders would
not leave him alone; they pressed him relentlessly: "Certainly
you are also one of them, for your accent betrays you." Peter
lost his head completely and began to curse and swear, "I do
not know the man." Immediately the cock crowed. And the
Lord turned and looked at Peter. Peter remembered in overwhelming horror that Jesus had foretold that before the cock
crowed Peter would deny him three times. Peter went out and
wept bitterly. It is generally understood that St. Mark's gospel
owed much to Peter. It is in that gospel that the story of Peter's
denials is spelled out emphatically.

The trial before Pilate, necessary for the Roman execution,
began with Pilate going out to the Jews and trying to "pass the
buck." But this mythical commodity was soon passing backward and forward. What was the accusation? asked Pilate.
They told him that they would not have delivered Jesus to him
if he was not "an evil doer." "All right then," said Pilate, "take
him yourselves and judge him by your own law." But the Jews

knew the answer to that one. They were not allowed by Roman law to put anyone to death, so the whole decision was Pilate's and no one else's.

Pilate now bent his mind to the problem. He went into the palace again and asked Jesus anew, "Are you the King of the Jews?" Jesus, after some verbal fencing, tried to explain that from his point of view this question, as understood by Pilate and the Jews, was really a nonquestion. "My kingship is not of this world." If it were, his servants would have been fighting to prevent his arrest. "But my kingship is not of the world." Pilate, puzzled but still seeking the truth, pressed the point: "So you are a king?" Jesus answered, "You say that I am a king." From Pilate's standpoint that was an affirmative answer. But Jesus went on to try to lift Pilate's eyes to a higher vision. "For this I was born, and for this I have come into the world, to bear witness to the truth. Everyone who is from the truth hears my voice." Pilate asked him, not stupidly, but equally not beginning to understanding him, "What is truth?"

Pilate was stimulated and puzzled and not at all inclined to surrender this interesting man to the fanatics who wanted to butcher him. He was not lacking in devices. When he heard that Jesus was a Galilean and belonged therefore to Herod's jurisdiction, he sent him across to Herod, who was himself in Jerusalem at the time. No doubt this was an attempt to shelve responsibility, but it was nothing worse. Herod was very glad to meet Jesus, "for he had long desired to see him, because he had heard about him" and was hoping to see some sign done by him. But Jesus refused to "do his tricks" in front of Herod to such an extent that he declined to answer him at all. Herod apparently laughed the whole thing off and used it as an opportunity for making up a quarrel with Pilate. The latter was no further on.

Pilate tried a new tactic. Again, he went to the Jews and said to them, "I find no crime in him. But you have a custom that I should release one man for you at the Passover; will you have me release for you the King of the Jews?" The crowd, probably influenced by the chief priests and their agents, roared back at him, "Not this man, but Barrabas." Barrabas was in fact a robber.

But Pilate had not yet finished with Jesus. Whether we are charitable or otherwise about his motives, he did persist in his efforts to release Jesus, prepared to try any means, however callous. He took Jesus and scourged him. "And the soldiers plaited a crown of thorns, and put it on his head, and arrayed him in a purple robe; they came up to him, saying, 'Hail, King of the Jews!' And struck him with their hands." Pilate then brought Jesus again before the crowd outside, still insisting that he found no crime in him. He exhibited him in his crown of thorns, purple robe, and humiliated condition, bruised and covered with spittle. Pointing to him before them all, he used the unforgettable though ambivalent words, "Behold the man!" (*Ecce homo!*).

Possibly he was making some appeal to their pity. But he was doubtless hoping also to show that this pitiable figure could constitute no threat to the Jewish authorities. On Pilate's lips the famous words might well have been taken to mean, "Look at the poor fellow."

The chief priests and their allies were not going to be out-witted in this way. They shouted ever more loudly, "Crucify him, crucify him!" Pilate told them yet again that he found "no crime in him." If they wanted to crucify him, they must take over the job themselves. The Jews answered with a solemn religious affirmation, "We have a law, and by that law he ought to die, because he made himself the Son of God."

We are told that at this point Pilate became "the more afraid." It was not the Jews who disturbed him so much as Jesus and the supernatural powers that conceivably resided in him. Pilate went back into the palace and asked Jesus: "Where are you from?" Jesus made no reply. Pilate asked him whether he did not realize that he, Pilate, had authority either to release him or crucify him—crucifixion was the normal form of

Roman execution for all except Roman citizens. Jesus commented: "You would have no power over me unless it had been given you from above; therefore he who delivered me to you has the greater sin." From that time, we are told, Pilate tried harder and harder to release him, for Jesus seemed to him anything but politically subversive.

But when Pilate began yet another plea to the crowd outside, he was shouted down with the cry: "If you release this man, you are not Caesar's friend; every one who makes himself a king sets himself against Caesar." Now at last they had found a language to cut through his resistance. Pilate's whole career, one might almost say his whole existence, depended on his standing well with Rome. He had clashed before with the Jews and dared not take another risk. Once he had set up ensigns bearing the effigy of the Emperor, an act idolatrous to the Jews. Another time riots had caused the removal of shields bearing Tiberius' name that had been hung in Herod's palace. Earlier, Pilate had put down with bloodshed a riot caused by the diversion of temple revenues. Pilate seems to have been a typical member of the Roman governing class, ultracivilized, for good or ill. It is generally argued that his dislike and contempt for the Jews gave him something of a bias toward Jesus.

By this time, he fully appreciated that Jesus' acceptance of the title King of the Jews offered no conceivable threat to Roman supremacy, but he also recognized that it could be made to look as though it did. He had fought quite hard, harder it may be than most of us would have fought in his situation, but now he had done all he could. He capitulated. For the first time he constituted his court of justice formally. He sat down upon a judgment seat in the place called Pavement or, in Hebrew, Gabbatha.

Jesus was brought before him, and Pilate indulged in a final jibe at the Jews' expense. Pointing to Jesus, he said to the Jews: "Behold your King." They shouted: "Away with him, away with him, crucify him!" Pilate said, perhaps smiling sarcastically, "Shall I crucify your King?" They answered confidently at last and, as always, self-righteously: "We have no king but Caesar." So Pilate delivered Jesus to them to be crucified.

*   *   *

The buffeting and spitting and mocking salutations were repeated. Jesus' clothes were restored to him, but the crown of thorns was left on his brow to continue the mockery.

He was led away accepting his cross, it is believed, with alacrity. But almost at once he faltered and fell. The beatings and other severities had reduced him to a physical wreck. Many have found symbolic meanings in this and the subsequent "Stations of the Cross." They see Jesus as representing here the pain and humiliation of all who break down much sooner than expected. Jesus staggered to his feet, and as he did so he saw his mother. It seems that no words passed between them. Their communion in suffering did not require them.

But even his insensitive guards could see that he would never complete the journey unaided. A man of Cyrene, called Simon, was drafted in to help him. He was clearly a conscript for the purpose. But we can surely believe that Simon, the only African mentioned in the gospels, looked back on this service with pride in after years.

A great multitude followed him, many sympathetic, some previous admirers who had turned contemptuous, and some hoping against hope for a miracle. Tradition has it that only one person, a woman called Veronica, showed positive and public compassion. She forced her way through the crowd and through the Roman soldiers and hastened to his side. By this time Jesus' face was unrecognizable. In Caryll Houselander's vivid description: "The eyes which could see into the secret places of men's souls were blinded, swollen from the long sleepless nights of trial and judgment, and filled with sweat and blood. The cheeks were bruised and dirty; the mouth swollen; the hair tangled by the crown of thorns, and matted with blood." Veronica knelt down; Jesus leaned toward her. She wiped his battered, disfigured face with a clean linen cloth. For a short while at least the blood and sweat and tears were dried. He could look into a face that reflected his own agony and his own radiance.

Another fall, in spite of the help of Simon. And now the women in the crowd were making no secret of their poignant sympathy. But he was concerned not with his own pain and sorrow, but with theirs. "Daughters of Jerusalem," he begged them, "do not weep for me, but weep for yourselves and for your children." The days were coming when the childless women would be reckoned as the lucky ones. Then they would begin to say to the mountains, "Fall on us," and to the hills, "Cover us."

Some surprise has been expressed that Jesus should appear to have refused such well-intentioned sympathy. Surely that was not in character? But he was looking ahead not only to the fall of Jerusalem, but also to the sufferings of all human beings, especially women, to the end of time.

He was now at the foot of the little hill of Calvary. A further fall, a further humiliation, awaited him. He collapsed for the third time and was dragged once more to his feet. At last he reached the summit. But another little ceremony had to be gone through, before the final atrocity. He was stripped of his clothing. "When the soldiers had crucified Jesus they took his garments and made four parts, one for each soldier; also his tunic. But the tunic was without seam, woven from top to bottom; so they said to one another, 'Let us not tear it, but cast lots for it to whose it shall be.'" A certain pedantry, a certain correctitude, persisted to the finish.

The gospel narrative describes the nailing to the cross starkly and simply. "So they took Jesus . . . to the place called the place of the skull, which is called in Hebrew Golgotha. There they crucified him, and with him two others, one on either side." Our imaginations must do the rest.

Meanwhile, Pilate had not said quite his last word to show his contempt for the Jewish leaders who had worsted him and compelled him to act against his better nature. "Pilate also wrote a title and put it on the cross; it read, 'Jesus of Nazareth, the King of the Jews.'" The Jews did not realize he was teasing them. "Do not write, 'The King of the Jews,'" they said to him, "but, 'This man said, I am King of the Jews.'" "What I have written I have written," replied Pilate, closing the subject. He had at least coined a historic phrase.

The crowd stood by "watching," judging it prudent to keep their sentiments hidden, but the "rulers" were now thoroughly enjoying themselves. They scoffed at Jesus openly, saying, "he saved others; let him save himself, if he is the Christ of God, the Chosen One." The soldiers were equally derisive. Jesus, hanging from the cross in mounting agony, thought first of the moral guilt of his persecutors. Not for a moment did he forget that they, like all other members of the human race, were his father's children. "Father," he prayed, "forgive them; for they know not what they do."

Both criminals beside him were outraged that one who claimed to be Christ should be so futile on his behalf and theirs: "Are you not the Christ?" they called to him. "Save yourself and us." But later on, one repented and rebuked the other. "Do you not fear God, since we are under the same sentence of condemnation?" In their own case it was perfectly just; they were guilty men. But Jesus was totally innocent. One prayer the man did feel entitled to offer respectfully. "Jesus," he said, "remember me when you come into your kingdom." Jesus replied with the firmest consolation ever offered to the dying, "Truly, I say to you, today you will be with me in Paradise."

Jesus was not totally deserted. Beside the cross was standing his mother; his mother's sister; Mary, the wife of Cleopas; and Mary Magdalene. And of the apostles, at least St. John. Jesus saw his mother and St. John, and an inspiration struck him. Pointing to St. John, he said to his mother, "Woman, your son."

And to St. John, "Behold, your mother." From that hour the disciple took her to his own house. He may in fact have led her away at once so that she should not have to endure the spectacle of the final agonies. By this time the sheer physical suffering must have been excruciating. The psychological torture of sharing the burden of the evil that prevailed at that moment is fortunately beyond our grasp.

About the ninth hour Jesus cried with a loud voice: *"Eli, Eli, lama sabachthani?"* or, in English, "My God, my God, why hast thou forsaken me?" It might seem that he was at that moment very near to despair. But it has been pointed out that he was quoting the first verse of Psalm 22, which ends on a note of triumph, and it may be that only the first words were caught by those standing around. But surely we must believe that he plumbed the depths of conceivable affliction. For a man or woman to feel deserted by God is terrible enough. It must have been a thousand times worse for a divine being.

The supreme horror passed, or rather was overcome. There came a moment when he knew that his course had been completed. "I thirst," he said. They filled a sponge with vinegar and, putting it on a javelin, lifted it to his mouth. He received it and drank the vinegar, perhaps to make sure that his faculties were undimmed at the culmination. When he had drunk the vinegar, he said: "It is finished," or in some translations, "consummated."

His last words made it clearer still that his mission was accomplished, his father's will carried out, his mind finally at peace; he could now return whence he came. "Father," he said, all sense of dereliction utterly banished, "Father, into thy hands I commit my spirit." Having said that, he breathed his last.

We only have glimpses of the bystanders' reactions, and St. Matthew and St. Mark tell us of the rending of the veil of the temple and other astonishing portents. The centurion and others "keeping watch over Jesus" were filled with awe and said: "Truly this was the Son of God." And there is a brief statement in St. Luke that all the multitudes who had come to see the sight "returned home beating their breasts."

* * *

At least one member of the council, Joseph of Arimethea, "a good and righteous man," had not supported the actions against Jesus. He now went to Pilate and asked for Jesus' body. On receiving permission, he took it away. Our old friend Nicodemus, "who had at first come to Jesus by night," brought an expensive mixture of myrrh and aloes. They wound the body of Jesus in linen cloths "with the spices," according to the recognized custom. "Now in the place where he was crucified there was a garden, and in the garden a new tomb where no one had ever been laid." There they laid Jesus with all care and reverence. The impending Sabbath made the burial hasty and perhaps provisional. The women who had come with Jesus from Galilee followed, and saw the tomb and how his body was laid; then they returned, and prepared spices and ointments for the body.

The Jewish leaders were genuinely fearful that the friends of Jesus might spirit away his body to substantiate his promise that he would rise on the third day. They demanded that Pilate should take adequate steps to make this impossible, but he had had enough of them for one day. He pointed out that there was already a guard, and it was up to them to see that it was made effective. So they went and made the sepulcher secure "by sealing the stone and setting a guard." They had taken every possible precaution against their human opponents.

12
Jesus Rises from the Dead

"Please send word to the Bishop of Chichester," said the martyr Bonhöffer, just before he was executed by the Nazis, "that for me this is not the end, but the beginning of life." So it was now for the disciples, that group of Galilean nobodies who, broken and discredited, were about to undergo experiences of the risen Christ that would inspire them to transform the course of world history. It was the cardinal belief of the early Christians that the Church they knew and loved was founded by the risen Christ. "If Christ has not risen, then our preaching is in vain and your faith is in vain," wrote St. Paul in his first letter to the Corinthians (I Cor. 15:14).

From the beginning, the disciples realized that the purpose of Christ's Resurrection was not primarily to make a miraculous demonstration but to rescue the entire human race. St. Peter wrote in his first "letter": "He himself bore our sins in his body on the tree, that we might die to sin and live to righteousness. By his wounds you have been healed." "For thou wast slain," wrote St. John, "and by thy blood didst ransom men for God, from every tribe and tongue and people and nation." The doctrines of the Crucifixion, the Resurrection, and the Atonement have all along been indissolubly connected. St. Paul summed it all up in the fifth chapter of his letter to the Romans: "For if while we were enemies we were reconciled to God by the death of his son, much more, now that we are reconciled, shall we be saved by his life."

It is clear that the Resurrection was not just a resuscitation of the human body of Jesus, nor merely the appearance of a ghost. His human body was transformed into a spiritual body that could, for example, withdraw itself from grave cloths, pass through closed doors, appear and disappear, and be recognized only with some difficulty. At the same time, Jesus could display the marks of his sufferings, which "doubting" Thomas could be invited to touch, and could reassure his disciples by eating before their eyes. All this we can accept readily enough, without laying claim to total comprehension. Here we are concerned not with metaphysics or semantics, but with elucidating the essential facts in their bearing on our human destiny.

St. Paul is worth quoting again on the Resurrection, if only because he recorded the events so soon after their happening. Paul, a Jew from Tarsus and a Roman citizen, had never encountered the living Jesus; Paul had been prominent for his persecution of the first Christians until his blinding vision of Christ on the road to Damascus, which changed his whole way of life. He would have heard of the Resurrection between two and eight years after it happened and written his first letter to Corinthians, which was not his first epistle, twenty years after that. At that point many who recollected the events at first hand would still have been alive.

Paul reminded the Corinthians of the message he had received and emphasized to them "that Christ died for our sins in accordance with the scriptures, that he was buried, that he was raised on the third day." He mentioned that Jesus appeared to Cephas (Peter), to the twelve, to more than five hundred brethren at one time, most of them then still alive, to James, and then to all the apostles again. "Last of all, as to one untimely born," adds St. Paul, "he appeared also to me." The fact that he placed the appearance to himself in the series with the others shows that he regarded them all as being of the same kind.

* * *

The accounts of the Resurrection by the different evangelists are not too difficult to harmonize, although at one or two points a biographer has only his own discretion to rely on.

At early dawn, on the first day of the week, Easter Sunday, three days after Good Friday, a number of women "who had come with him from Galilee" (St. Luke) made their way to the tomb, carrying spices to anoint the body. The evangelist makes specific mention of Mary Magdalene and Mary the mother of James, Salome, and Joanna. One may suppose that there were at least six of them altogether and possibly more. Their immediate problem (St. Matthew) was how to roll back the heavy stone at the mouth of the tomb. But it was solved, to their astonishment and that of the guards on duty, by "an angel of the Lord," who rolled back the stone and "sat upon it." He told the women to put aside their fears. Jesus whom they were looking for was not there, "for he has risen, as he said."

The angel showed them the place now empty that Jesus had occupied, and bade them report what they had heard to the apostles. They set off for the city, but on the way another and still greater shock awaited them. Jesus himself appeared before them, with the simple greeting "Hail!"

There is need for a little ingenuity to reconcile the account just given with that of St. John, in which Mary Magdalene appears at first to come alone to the tomb. However, it is not hard to find an explanation that does not invalidate the claim that Mary was the first to see the risen Jesus. Mary would seem to have accompanied the other women to the tomb, but, seeing the stone rolled back and without waiting further, dashed off, on fire with excitement, to tell Peter and John. All three of them then made their way to the tomb, John outrunning Peter, and Mary bringing up the rear. John, stopping to look inside, saw the linen cloths there, but did not venture in. Peter, always the boldest of the bold, had no qualms, and went straight into the tomb. "He saw the linen cloths lying, and the napkin, which had been on his head, not lying with the linen cloths but rolled up in a place by itself." Then John himself, who is our authority for this story, "also went in, and he saw and believed." We are told, rather surprisingly, that "as yet they did not know the scripture, that he must rise from the dead." But it was not for want of Jesus telling them. The sight of the discarded garments was necessary to convince them of the supernatural happening. They then went back to their homes.

Mary Magdalene stood outside the tomb, weeping, but she could not refrain from stooping down and looking in. She saw two angels in white, who asked her why she was weeping, and she replied simply and completely: "Because they have taken away my Lord and I do not know where they have laid him." At that moment, however, she turned around "and saw Jesus standing, but she did not know that it was Jesus." He also asked her why she was weeping and whom she was looking for—though, of course, he did not need her to tell him the answer. She replied respectfully but piteously, "Sir, if you have carried him away, tell me where you have laid him, and I will take him away." Still she did not recognize him, perhaps because of the darkness, perhaps because her vision was obscured by tears, perhaps because she was speaking over her shoulder, or perhaps because he did not look quite the same as before his Resurrection. In a different tone, perhaps softer and more affectionate, he said one word, "Mary!" That was enough. She turned and said to him in Hebrew, "Rabboni!" (which can be translated "Teacher" or "Master"). Jesus said to her, "Do not hold me, for I have not yet ascended to the Father"—another of his cryptic sayings. She was to go to his "brethren" and say to them that he was ascending to his father and their father, to his God and their God. Mary hastened off and said to the disciples, "I have seen the Lord," but it is doubtful how far they believed her.

Later that day (St. Luke), two of Jesus' followers, one of them called Cleopas, were walking to Emmaus, a village about seven miles from Jerusalem. A stranger fell into step beside them. It was Jesus, although they did not recognize him (not the first or last example of nonrecognition after he had risen). He asked what they were talking about. "And they stood still, looking sad." Then Cleopas burst out incredulously: Their new acquaintance must have been the only visitor to Jerusalem not aware of the extraordinary happenings of the past few days. Jesus innocently drew them on with further questions. They told him that they were referring to Jesus of Nazareth, a prophet "mighty in words and deed." The chief priests and rulers had seized and crucified him. It had been a crushing blow, for they had hoped that he was the one to redeem Israel. Yet they did not seem to have quite despaired. They seemed to recall his statement that he would rise again on the third day, and that very morning, the third morning since the Crucifixion, some women of their company had found the tomb empty. There were rumors, moreover, of a vision of angels who said that he was alive. This news appeared to have been confirmed. Jesus spoke to them with seeming roughness but obviously not in a way to cause offense. Didn't they realize that all this was in accordance with the classical prophecies? Was it not necessary that Christ should suffer these things and enter into his glory? He went on to interpret to them "in all the scriptures the things concerning himself."

It was getting late, so when they reached their destination, they begged him to stay with them. Clearly he fascinated them, though they still had no idea who he was. "When he was at table with them, he took the bread and blessed, and broke it, and gave it to them," and now at last the veil was removed from their eyes. They saw that it was Jesus, but at that moment he vanished from their sight.

We can assume that the two covered the seven miles back to Jerusalem in record time. They found the apostles and others gathered together with startling news of their own: "The Lord has risen indeed, and has appeared to Simon" (this appearance is no doubt that referred to by St. Paul in I Corinthians 15, but we know nothing more of it). Cleopas and his friend had much to tell them in an atmosphere of dawning hopefulness. The Emmaus story comes from St. Luke, but we must turn to St. John for the clearest picture of the evening in Jerusalem when Jesus appeared to the apostles.

The doors being shut "for fear of the Jews," Jesus came and stood among them and said to them, "Peace be with you." When he had said this he showed them his hands and his side. The disciples were overjoyed. It is impossible not to think that he responded fully to their happiness, but he was concerned as always with the task ahead. "As the Father has sent me," he said, "even so I send you." Then he "breathed on them" and said to them, "Receive the Holy Spirit. If you forgive the sins of any, they are forgiven; if you retain the sins of any, they are retained."

It happened that Thomas was not with them when Jesus came. The other disciples told him, "We have seen the Lord," but Thomas was skeptical. "I will not believe," he said, "unless I see in his hands the print of the nails, and place my finger in the mark of the nails, and place my hand in his side." He soon had his doubts set at rest.

Eight days later the disciples were together again, and Thomas this time was with them. The doors were shut, but Jesus it seems passed through them. He stood among them and again said, "Peace be with you." He singled out Thomas for attention, well aware of the precise form his doubts had taken. "Put your finger here," he said, "and see my hands; and put out your hand, and place it in my side." Thomas should be no longer faithless, but believing.

Thomas answered with unreserved acceptance, "My Lord and my God!" Jesus did not fail to point out the moral. It was all very well that Thomas should believe because of what he had seen, but "Blessed are those who have not seen and yet believe."

There were three more recorded appearances: two in Galilee, one in Jerusalem. The last one, it would seem, was more sustained than the other two.

We learn from St. Matthew that the eleven disciples went to Galilee "to the mountain to which Jesus had directed them." Jesus came to them and gave them perhaps the most emphatic of all their directives. "All authority in heaven and on earth," he said, "has been given to me." He laid on them the solemn duty to "make disciples of all nations." They should baptize them "in the name of the Father and of the Son and of the Holy Spirit, teaching them to observe all that I have commanded you." His last words provided limitless assurance: "and lo, I am with you always, to the close of the age."

The final scene by the lake in Galilee recalls the happiness of the earlier ministry. Half a dozen of the apostles were together: "Simon Peter, Thomas called the Twin, Nathanael of Cana in Galilee, the sons of Zebedee, and two others of his disciples." They had been out on the lake fishing all night. By morning they had caught nothing. Just as day was breaking, Jesus stood on the beach; yet the disciples did not know that it was Jesus. "Children," asked this unknown figure, possessed it would seem of a peculiar authority, "have you any fish?" They told him they had none. He told them to cast their net on the right side of the boat. They did so and suddenly they found that they had far more fish than they could manage. John, "the disciple whom Jesus loved," then realized the truth. "It is the Lord," he exclaimed. Peter needed no further signal: He plunged into the sea and swam to Jesus, while the others brought in the mighty haul.

Already Jesus had a charcoal fire burning "with fish lying on it and bread." Some of the 153 fish that had just been caught were prepared, and a hearty breakfast was enjoyed by all. "Jesus came and took the bread and gave it to them, and so with the fish." Jesus seldom failed to give a material occasion a spiritual meaning.

It was not long since Peter had made his three heart-rending denials. Now he was given the chance to cancel them out, at this stage in words and later on in deeds. Three questions were put to Peter, and he gave three answers. Whatever the original words used by Jesus and Peter in Aramaic, the Greek versions in the gospels have given rise to various translations into English. We cannot do better than follow Archbishop Temple (with some adaptations). Jesus said to Peter, "Simon, son of John, do you love me more than these?" Peter replied, "Yes, Lord; you know that I am your friend." He said to him, "Feed my lambs." He said to him again a second time, "Simon, son of John, do you love me?" Peter replied, "Yes, Lord, you know that I am your friend." Jesus said to him, "Tend my sheep." He then said to him the third time, "Simon, son of John, are you my friend?" Peter said, "Lord, you know all things; you see that I am your friend." Jesus said, "Feed my sheep."

His questions follow a declining scale. Do you love me more than these? Do you love me? Are you my friend? But the commissions follow an ascending scale: feed my lambs; tend my sheep; feed my sheep (each of the last two phrases covering more than its predecessor). We must assume that these delicate nuances were fully appreciated by Peter and that, utterly humiliated by his previous failure, he was aware that he was being paid the supreme compliment of being singled out for unlimited responsibilities. No one can fail to notice the humility, one might say the timidity, of Peter's answers. He had so recently and so lamentably failed his beloved master. He would not lay claim to any form of devotion stronger than friendship. Jesus understood him perfectly. Jesus then went on to use words which, according to the evangelist, signified the manner of death by which Peter would glorify God. He then said to him: "Follow me," and when Peter asked about St. John's destiny, set the question aside with the repeated, "Follow me!"

Tradition has it that Peter escaped from his prison in Rome the night before he was due to be executed. He was fleeing along the Appian Way when he met Jesus carrying a cross. "Lord," he asked, "where are you going?" (*Domine, quo vadis?*) "I am going," said Jesus, "to Rome to be crucified afresh." Peter would have been the last man in the world to miss the point of the delicate correction. He turned forthwith and made his way back to prison and martyrdom insisting, we are told, on being crucified head downward, so as not to place himself on a par with his master. Jesus' last words to Peter ("Follow me") were, this time, carried out to the death.

And so back to Jerusalem for the last scene of all. It was forty days since the Resurrection. Now, St. Luke tells us, Jesus opened their minds—at last he thought they were equipped to understand the scriptures. "Thus it is written," he said, "that the Christ should suffer and on the third day rise from the dead, and that repentance and forgiveness of sins should be preached in his name to all nations beginning from Jerusalem." So for the last time, clearly and unequivocally, they were instructed to preach the Christian message to all men. "And behold," he said, "I send the promise of my Father upon you." But they were to stay in the city until they were clothed with power from on high. Then he led them out as far as Bethany and delivered his final message: "You shall receive power," he said, "when the Holy Spirit has come upon you; and you shall be my witnesses in Jerusalem and in all the earth." Then he blessed them and, in the very act of doing so, was carried up into heaven. "And they returned to Jerusalem with great joy and were continually in the temple blessing God."

They had not very long to wait. "When the Day of Pentecost had come," a few days after the Ascension, "they were all together in one place." Suddenly a sound came from heaven "like the rush of a mighty wind," which filled the whole house. Tongues of fire descended on them. They were all filled with the Holy Spirit "and began to speak in other tongues as the Spirit gave them utterance."

From that moment they set off, with total self-confidence and complete disregard for their personal safety, to spread the gospel throughout the known world. In almost every quarter of it they laid down their lives, and the blood of the martyrs was indeed "the seed of the Church." They, if any group of men would have been, were entitled to apply to themselves the ancient inscription, "If you want our monument, look around you." But it would have been about the last text they would have thought of using. It was above all not their own monument that they were given strength and faith to establish.

13
Jesus' Message

Those, briefly, and allowing for reasonable varieties of emphasis, are the facts of Jesus' life. What light do they throw on his message? The late H. A. L. Fisher, an uncompromising rationalist, referred in his history of Europe to the "cleansing tide of Christian ethics" as one of the most glorious features of European history. Some who are reluctant to call themselves Christians, but are public-spirited citizens, will say that they accept these same Christian ethics, but not the theology or the "mumbo jumbo."

Yet the more closely one looks into the teaching and story of Christ, the more impossible it is by any process of honest thought to separate the ethics from the theology, or either or both from the life. Non-Christians who say they accept the Christian ethic usually mean in practice that they accept the second commandment: You shall love your neighbor as yourself. Jesus gave this well-known formula from Leviticus a new and universal meaning in the parable of the good Samaritan and in his firm injunction that we must love not only our friends, but also our enemies.

It was not, however, the mere words that gave that teaching its historical influence so that, in Matthew Arnold's words, it "lighted up morality." Jesus said in his last discourse, "You must love each other as I have loved you," but that instruction has derived its tremendous inspiration from his personality (including his divine claims), as his disciples knew him and as we have come to know him.

The distinguished Jewish Professor Geza Vermes has produced a convincing tribute to the ethics introduced by Jesus in his book *Jesus the Jew*. He calls Jesus helper and healer, teacher and leader, to be venerated as a prophet, Son of God. That last phrase is used somewhat restrictedly. It was not to be expected that he would recognize Jesus as God in the Christian sense. He sees him rather as one of the venerable company of the devout, the ancient Hasidim. But as compared with the other members of that company, he boldly states that "no objective and enlightened student of the Gospels can help but be struck by the incomparable superiority of Jesus." He quotes another and earlier Jewish authority: "In his ethical code there is a sublimity, distinctiveness, and originality in form, unparalleled in any other Hebrew ethical code; neither is there any parallel to the remarkable art of his parables."

And he goes farther in his generous estimate. "In one respect more than in any other," he says, "he differed from both his contemporaries and even his prophetic predecessors. The prophets had indeed spoken on behalf of the poor, the oppressed, and the exploited, but Jesus did not confine himself to words; he actually took his stand among the pariahs of this world, those despised by the respectable. Sinners were his table companions and the ostracized tax collectors and prostitutes, his friends." Professor Vermes confirms what is, indeed, hardly doubtful, that you cannot separate, except for purposes of discussion, the life, the ethics, and the theology of Jesus—although admittedly Professor Vermes does stop short of the Christian theological position.

Altruism, in one form or another, is propounded by most of the great philosophies and theologies. Confucius, for example, presented the yen as the key to his moral philosophy, and said of it: "Yen is to love all men. The man of yen is called a superior man." Picking up the Roman Stoic philosopher, Seneca, almost at random one finds: "Treat your inferiors in the way in which you would like to be greeted by your own superiors." Mahomet drew much from Christian sources. But certain features of the love enjoined by Jesus must be taken as a connected pattern. It should not be based on a mere enlightened self-interest. On the contrary, it should be utterly self-forgetful and overlook entirely the possible lack of merit in the recipient. Above all, it should reflect an inner attitude. In the Sermon on the Mount, for example, murder, adultery, divorce, perjury, and revenge are all traced to inner attitudes, and so are the less obvious products of the attitudes in question—anger, lust, and so on. But with the help of God, the inner attitudes can be utterly transformed.

Yet surely one must look farther for the three most distinctive marks of Christian ethics. Are they not humility, forgiveness, and a spiritual view of suffering? Here again, we encounter simultaneously the ethics, the theology, and the example of Jesus. Christian humility, as the present writer has said elsewhere, begins with Christ. In a sense it ends there. The Christian debt to Plato and Aristotle is permanent, but not in regard to humility.

Humility involves at least five distinguishable ideas: knowledge of oneself as one is, in the face of God and one's fellow men; the rejection of pride; meekness; obedience; and service. But those who try to live a life of humility will turn primarily to the whole life and death of Christ, as a superlative example of the virtue. Perhaps St. Paul puts the point most clearly (in his letter to the Philippians [2, 6–8]): Jesus, "though he was in the form of God, did not count equality with God a thing to be grasped, but emptied himself, taking the form of a servant, being born in the likeness of men. And being found in human form he humbled himself and became obedient unto death, even death on a cross."

When Jesus said to Peter that he should forgive his brother up to seventy times seven, he was in a sense laying down an abstract proposition. In the parable of the prodigal son, he was teaching through an imaginative fable. But there was nothing abstract or imaginative when he prayed for his tormentors from the cross. "Father, forgive them, for they know not what they do"; or when he gave the penitent thief the assurance "This day you will be with me in paradise." Every time a Christian says the "Our Father," he uses the words "Forgive us our trespasses, as we forgive them who trespass against us." Christianity and forgiveness are so wrapped up together that they cannot be separated. Nor can the abstractions be separated from the life's performance of their divine author.

The existence of suffering, like that of evil, has throughout the ages caused torment and bewilderment to sensitive minds. Not least to the Jews, as we are aware from the Book of Job. The world has never lacked good men and women, anxious to relieve the sufferings of others, and to accept with serenity their own. But the central question has remained why suffering, like evil, is permitted. Today, detestation of suffering goes hand in hand with widespread man-inflicted suffering in new and horrific forms. The age-long problem of how so much evil and suffering in the world can be reconciled with the existence of an all-powerful and loving God is probably the greatest single barrier to religious belief; it seems to make it so much harder to love God in any genuine sense. To love God adequately is beyond the power of our fallen human nature, but no one, surely, of sensitive spirit can fail to love God a little more than hitherto, as he reads and rereads the gospel story. In other words, the historical is highly relevant to the religious conclusion.

Can one believe that the facts recorded here are true—that God did indeed become man and died in agony on the cross to save the human race? If we can, the possibility that God is beneficent, in spite of many bewildering phenomena, is inevitably very much strengthened. It is the Resurrection that helps us most to believe that God is all-powerful, the Crucifixion that he is all-loving.

Even after two thousand years of Christianity, an element of mystery continues. But Christianity has provided an altogether more profound meaning to redemptive or creative suffering. This is the suffering that we ourselves accept in such a fashion that others may benefit. Yet here again, one cannot distinguish sharply between the teaching of Jesus and the significance of his life, death, and example. The doctrine of suffering is barely adumbrated in the Sermon on the Mount. But as the time drew near for his own supreme sacrifice, he warned his disciples ever more plainly that suffering is the law of life; that self-sacrifice, even self-immolation, is necessary to self-fulfillment and to the "bearing of much fruit."

Past attempts to separate the moral teaching from the claims of Jesus to divinity have never succeeded, even when undertaken by a man of genius like Renan in the past century. The dilemma before a rationalist who pursues this line is surely beyond solution. It can be stated in simple terms. No other founder or leader of a great religion claimed to be divine; Jesus did so. We must assume *ex hypothesi* his good faith. We are left then to conclude that he was, or became, totally demented, presenting a claim that would render him a suitable candidate for a mental home. The rationalist is left muttering that whatever one may say, things like that—like the life, death, and Resurrection of Jesus Christ—just don't happen. And yet if we once accept the possibility that God exists, we can readily accept the further possibility that he became incarnate, and, in that case, one would expect the events of his life to be unlike those of any other, before or since.

If at this point the rationalist turns the discussion a little onto the ground of comparative religion, where quite a lot of faith was lost at one time, one can only make the now familiar point that the other stories of gods who died and rose again cannot be fairly compared with the life story of Christ. By common consent Jesus lived and died during a definite period of recorded history.

But is one trying to prove too much, to bring reason farther than is justified in support of faith? Is one saying that the essentials of Christ's life, ethics, and theology can all be discovered on the face of the gospels by a dispassionate and intelligent student? As regards the life and ethics—yes. As regards the theology, not quite, but almost.

Anyone who works at the gospels as earnestly as he would at an academic text should get at least as far in his appreciation of Jesus' relationship with God the Father as Professor Vermes, quoted earlier. Indeed, he should be able to get a little farther. Professor Vermes, after careful consideration, plays down the messiahship of Jesus. Christians are entitled to turn to the last verse of John 20 and accept its message. We are told there that these signs were described "that you may believe that Jesus is the Christ, the Son of God, and that believing you may have life in his name." But today few non-Jewish readers, unless they have a special interest in biblical history, are primarily concerned with a messianic claim one way or the other.

Do the gospels really teach us beyond reasonable doubt that Jesus was God in the accepted Christian sense? In other words, do they demonstrate irresistibly the claim made in the Creed that "he is the only-begotten Son of God, begotten of his Father before all worlds, being of one substance with the Father by whom all things were made . . ."? It would be hard to say that, if one started afresh, one would automatically reach those conclusions; but after two thousand years of theological investigation and religious education, it is not difficult to accept them.

Matthew, Mark, and Luke carry the matter a certain distance. The angel at the time of the Annunciation said to Mary: "The child to be born will be called holy, the Son of God." We are told that Jesus said to the tempter: "It is written: 'You shall not tempt the Lord your God.'" But in St. John we find a clear recognition that Jesus was divine in the full sense. After Jesus' Resurrection, Thomas hails him without contradiction as "My Lord and my God!" Jesus himself said, "I and my Father are one."

Some Christians will speak in terms of the whole truth gradually emerging as the Holy Spirit worked on the collective mind of the Church. Others will be secure in the conviction that the Holy Spirit has brought them this personal message. Most Christians who are in any degree orthodox believe that Jesus founded a church, and he conferred on it powers to develop and spell out the message he left behind with his immediate disciples. Here everyone must speak for himself. For my part, I find no strain on loyalty—very much the reverse—in accepting the formulation of the Creed about the divinity of Christ. It seems to flow so naturally, indeed, inevitably from what is written in the gospels. In St. John, of course, most obviously; but not only in St. John.

These, however, are not the considerations that concern most of those whose lives are dedicated to Jesus Christ. With a growing world population, their number is probably greater today than at any time in world history. They are men and women of all sorts and conditions. "There," said a priest to me, as Sir Stafford Cripps finished a noble oration at the Albert Hall, "there goes a man with an immense love of our Lord." The same can be said of many who in our time have labored all over the world in the cause of the afflicted, from Mother Teresa, Bishop Trevor Huddleston, Leonard Cheshire, and the late Martin Luther King downward; and of countless others who are themselves the afflicted; and of the still larger numbers who live what are called ordinary lives.

"Come unto me all you who labor and are heavy burdened and I will give you rest. Take my yoke upon you and learn of me, for I am meek and humble of heart and you will find rest for your souls. For my yoke is sweet and my burden is light." Jesus speaks, as he has always spoken, to all men and women and children, saints and sinners, rich and poor, Christian and non-Christian. There are a hundred or a thousand different ways of finding him, but the most direct and obvious is to read what he said and did and suffered on our behalf, and to ponder upon the expression of his love.

CHRONOLOGICAL NOTE
by Father Corbishley

Our modern practice of using the B.C./A.D. dating was not devised until the sixth century. We have no absolutely certain indications of the precise dating of the events of Our Lord's life, though it is highly probable that the Crucifixion occurred either in the year 30 or the year A.D. 33. (The arguments for determining this are rather too specialized and complicated for this book.) However, the author has assumed that the Crucifixion is to be dated to A.D. 30, and has based his chronology of the public life on this assumption. The precise dating does not, of course, matter, but it is important that readers should recognize that these events did happen at a definite moment in history.

Selected Bibliography

Anderson, Professor J.N.D. *A Lawyer Among the Theologians.* London: Hodder & Stoughton, 1973.
——. *Christianity: The Witness of History.* Wheaton, Ill.: Tyndale House, 1969.
Daniel-Rops, Henri. *Jesus in His Time,* trans. R. W. Millar. New York: Dutton, 1955.
Dodd, Professor C.H. *The Founder of Christianity.* London: Macmillan, 1970.
Goodier, Archbishop Alban. *The Passion and Death of Our Lord Jesus Christ.* Kenedy, 1933.
——. *The Public Life of Our Lord Jesus Christ: An Interpretation.* Kenedy, 1930.
Harvey, A.E. *Companion to the Gospels.* Cambridge, Eng.: Cambridge University Press, 1972.
McCulloch, Rev. Joseph. *Between God and Man.* London: Hutchinson, 1960.
Muggeridge, Malcolm. *Jesus Rediscovered.* Garden City, N.Y.: Doubleday, 1969.
Renan, E. *Life of Jesus.* London, 1863.
Sheed, Francis Joseph. *To Know Jesus Christ.* New York: Sheed & Ward, 1972.
Sheen, Bishop Fulton John. *Life of Christ.* New York: McGraw-Hill, 1958.
Temple, Archbishop William. *Readings in St. John's Gospel.* London: Macmillan, 1961.
Vermes, Geza. *Jesus the Jew.* London: Collins, 1973.